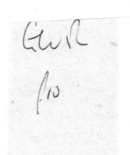

SWINDON
and the GWR

This book belongs to

RUSSELL JENNINGS.

SWINDON
and the GWR

Richard Tomkins and Peter Sheldon

ALAN SUTTON
and
REDBRICK
in association with
the Great Western Railway Museum, Swindon

First published in the United Kingdom in 1990 by
Alan Sutton Publishing Limited · Phoenix Mill · Stroud · Gloucestershire
and Redbrick Publishing · 38 Overbrook · Swindon · Wiltshire
in association with the Great Western Railway Museum, Swindon

First published in the United States of America in 1991 by
Alan Sutton Publishing Inc · Wolfeboro Falls · NH 03896–0848

British Library Cataloguing in Publication Data

Tomkins, Richard *1957–*
Swindon and the GWR
1. Wiltshire. Swindon. Railway services. Great Western Railway, history
I. Title   II. Sheldon, Peter *1946–*
385.0942313

ISBN 0–86299–790–9

Library of Congress Cataloging in Publication Data applied for

Typeset in 11/13 Bembo
Typesetting and origination by
Alan Sutton Publishing Limited.
Printed in Great Britain by
Dotesios Printers Limited.

Contents

Swindon stock shed, March 1920, looking north-east towards the gas works, with a terrace of houses in Ferndale Road just visible to the right. Engines are outside-framed pannier-tank No. 1282 fitted with spark-arrester (originally built in 1877 as a 'Buffalo' class saddle-tank similar to No. 1601 illustrated on p. 76), 'Bulldog' class No. 3359 *Tregeagle*, and an unidentified ROD 2–8–0 locomotive

Preface

Swindon and the GWR is a visual record of a railway town from all its aspects: factory, town and community. For many years Swindon was the Great Western Railway, the embodiment of an organization which embraced the best of Victorian enterprise and achievement. Although the Great Western has long since gone and the railway works are closed, the town will always retain a reflected image of the times when its name was synonymous with the highest standards of craftsmanship and reliability.

This book aims to evoke memories of the golden years of the GWR and its successor, the Western Region of British Railways, during the steam era. Compiled largely from the archives of the GWR Museum, the publication of this book comes during the year in which a major railway heritage exhibition is established within the precincts of the old GWR Works. *Swindon and the GWR* will help to provide the exhibition with an historical perspective and will, hopefully, appeal to local people with only a mild curiosity for the town's past, as well as the more diehard Great Western aficionados.

The photographs in the book, many published for the first time, reveal the wide-ranging influence of the GWR on the town and the vast infrastructure which was established to produce and maintain its magnificent railway engines and rolling-stock. From the mundane to the extraordinary, from everyday sights to special occasions, this compilation provides a unique glimpse of a not-too-distant past that is now gone forever.

Richard Tomkins
Peter Sheldon

Railwaymen and women of Swindon watch the naming ceremony of No. 92220 *Evening Star* in 'A' Shop, 18 March 1960. Broad-gauge locomotive *North Star* and diesel-hydraulic 'Warship' class No. D818 *Glory* provide examples of motive power spanning 120 years

Introduction

Without doubt, Swindon owes much of its fame to Isambard Kingdom Brunel's Great Western Railway. The extensive workshops established by the company in 1843 have dominated the economic, social and political life of the town for nearly one hundred and fifty years. Situated some eighty miles from London along Brunel's 'billiard table' main line, Swindon has long been the archetypal 'railway town', an image it has had great difficulty in shaking off, even in recent years, with the closure of the Works and the development of a wealth of new industries which have helped make the area one of the fastest growing in Western Europe.

The opening of a new railway works on green fields near the junction of the Great Western main line and the Cheltenham & Great Western Union Railway branch irrevocably changed the history of the small market town of Swindon situated on the hill above the railway line. As the years passed it became swamped by an entirely new community which grew up around the railway works, although the two townships were not to be fully united until 1900, when the Borough of Swindon was formally created.

No doubt the residents of Old Swindon looked on with some anxiety as the railway works grew in size and output as the century rolled on; when the operation began in January 1843 it was only intended as a repair and maintenance facility, but under the influence of the Great Western's Locomotive Superintendent, Daniel Gooch, construction of locomotives began in 1846. Further development took place in 1868, when the GWR chose Swindon as the site for its Carriage and Wagon Works.

Only a few years after this event, Swindon presided over a more sombre event, the destruction of Brunel's broad gauge. After 1870 an increasing number of 7 ft gauge locomotives and rolling stock were brought to the Works for breaking up; when the final conversion of the main line took place in May 1892, 195 locomotives, 748 passenger vehicles and 3,400 goods wagons were concentrated at Swindon for rebuilding or scrapping.

In the years after 1900, under the influence of George Jackson Churchward, the company's Locomotive Carriage and Wagon Superintendent, a stream of new and powerful locomotives emerged from Swindon Works, giving it a reputation second to none among the railways of Britain.

By the outbreak of the First World War, Swindon Works had become the heart of the Great Western system, producing almost everything needed by the company to run its operation. As well as the locomotives, carriages and wagons, Swindon craftsmen also turned out smaller items such as road vehicles, furniture, notices, lamps, tools and a host of other fittings all indelibly stamped with the company's initials.

The high standards set in the Churchward era were continued in the years after the First World War; arguably the most well-known Swindon products were turned out of the Works during this periods; the 'Castle' and 'King' designs came to be the mainstays of the

GWR express services until well after the Second World War. The inter-war years were not without their problems, however, as the world wide depression had its effects on the company's business.

In both world wars the railway works played a key role in the production of armaments and other items for the war effort. The efforts made by Swindon to recover from the struggles of the 1939–45 conflict were, however, interrupted by the nationalization of railways in 1948, when the Great Western became British Railways (Western Region). Much GWR tradition was carried on well into the British Railways era, but with the end of steam the operation gradually declined in size. In 1986, after much debate and heartache, the closure of Swindon Works, an event which many Swindonians thought would never happen, finally took place.

The purpose of this book is to evoke memories of happier times for the railway community in Swindon; for it is important to remember that Swindon was more than just a railway works. In the years before the Second World War, the life of the whole town was dominated by the company's operation; the physical extent of the factory, surrounded on most sides by great brick or stone walls, made it a closed world to all but those who were 'inside', as Swindonians called those who were employed in the Works.

With the opening of the new Works, a whole new community grew up around the company's site. There was no tradition of heavy engineering in this part of north Wiltshire, and the GWR was obliged to find labour from elsewhere, particularly in the case of skilled artisans, many of whom came to Swindon from other areas where railway engineering had already developed, such as Scotland and the north of England.

The company arranged for the buiding of what became known as the 'railway village', an estate of cottages laid out to the south of the GWR main line. Although well constructed by the standards of the time, initially the combination of poor sanitation, overcrowding and a dubious water supply led to the village being a rather unhealthy place to live.

Further housing grew up as the Works expanded, much of it constructed by speculative builders; green fields soon disappearing to be replaced by red-brick terraces housing more and more railway workers and their families. By 1900 New Swindon had grown to the extent that it became necessary to unite it with the 'old' Swindon community up on the hill. It was not coincidental that G.J. Churchward became the new borough's first mayor.

A whole range of facilities grew up as a result of the establishment of New Swindon, the company assisting in the provision of a school for the children of its work-force, situated in Bristol Street, and later replaced by local Board schools.

One of the most important developments was the setting up of the Mechanics Institute in 1843. It began life with the establishment of a library of books which had been purchased or donated by interested members, including Sir Daniel Gooch, and came to be the social, cultural and educational heart of the community. After holding events in the Works itself for some years, the Institute eventually acquired its own building situated on land leased from the GWR for a nominal sum. This, along with a market, was opened in 1855.

In 1892 the Institute building was further extended and by the turn of the century housed a theatre, library and reading rooms, billiards, chess and draughts rooms as well as various other meeting rooms where numerous clubs, societies and classes could meet.

The poor sanitary conditions already mentioned led to the setting up of the GWR Medical Fund in 1847. In its earliest form it enabled a doctor to be provided in the railway village, who was funded by weekly contributions from the pay of the Swindon work-force. As the Society developed it came to encompass a wide range of medical facilities, including a hospital, baths, a pharmacy, dentists, doctors and chiropodists. Such was its 'cradle to the grave' service, that it was said to have been one of the models for the National Health Service when it was being set up after the Second World War.

Finally, we cannot leave our survey of Swindon's railway heritage without mentioning two well-loved features of life in the town; the first, held in the GWR Park in Faringdon Road every summer, was the Children's Fête, organized by the Mechanics Institute, which enabled literally thousands of local children to enjoy both a slice of fruit cake and a ride on a fairground roundabout. The second was the annual Trip holiday, which dominated the family calendar each year: the company issued a free ticket for each employee and his family, which enabled them to go to the destination of their choice. Many chose the same resort, Weymouth, which many called 'Swindon by the Sea' although those who could afford it often went further. Both these Swindon institutions are portrayed, among many others, in this book.

The brief introduction given here to the development of Swindon as a railway community cannot do justice to the century and a half of history which has passed since the establishment of the Works at Swindon in 1843. Furthermore, it cannot hope to convey the part played in the story by the people of Swindon themselves, although hopefully something of the atmosphere of the place will come across in many of the evocative photographs reproduced here.

Most of the pictures assembled for this book come from the collection of the Great Western Railway Museum, Swindon and, as such, the book does not attempt to be a comprehensive survey of the Great Western's operation in the town. However, we do hope that this collection reveals something of the spirit of those who helped to build the giants of steam which emerged from Swindon's railway works, and evokes a time when Swindon truly was a 'Great Western Town'.

Tim Bryan, Keeper
Great Western Railway Museum, Swindon

Contemporary map of Swindon, 1880s, showing the extent of urban development and the dominance of the railway workshops in New Swindon. At that time, Old and New Swindon were separate communities, and were to remain so until the formation of the Borough of Swindon in 1900

The Railway Works in 1880

This fine series of workshop portraits is taken from a privately-produced photographic volume entitled *An Album of Photographic Views of the GWR Workshops*. Published by the firm of R.H. Bleasdale of Birmingham in the early 1880s, the views are designed to give a guided tour of 'one of the most extensive and celebrated locomotive factories in Europe'.

The locomotive erecting shop, as extended in the 1870s

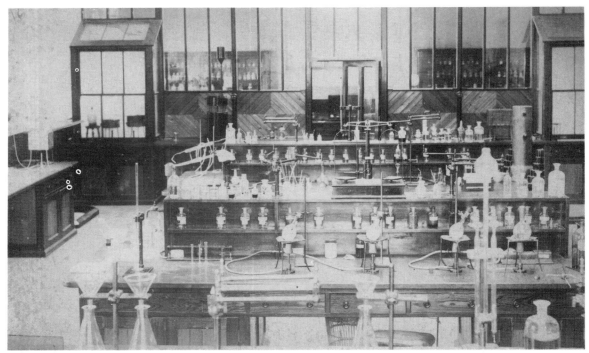

The chemical laboratory, housed in the former Bristol Street school extension and established by William Dean

The dining hall

The boiler shop, sited to the north of the iron foundry, adjoining Rodbourne Road

The carpenters and van shop in the original Carriage Works to the south of the line. Horse-drawn carts and vans are shown under construction in the background, while nearer the camera is a wide variety of wooden railway items: platform trolleys, hand-carts, wheels, a gas-lamp carrier, wheelbarrows and station benches marked with the names of Loudwater, Resolven, Carmarthen and Barbersbridge

The carriage erecting shop, housed in the same building as the carpenters shop, as can be seen from the foreman's office, which is also visible in the previous photograph

The carriage and wagon trimming shop

5

The sewing room

The leather shop

The millwrights shop, housed in the original 1842 boiler shop

The smiths shop

The pattern makers shop

The iron foundry, to the east of Rodbourne Road

Working Inside

The smiths shop: hammermen of Swindon stand proudly at their anvil, date unknown

The road motor shop. The back of this photograph is marked 'To Ethel, with love, 27/1/1920'

Snapshot view of employees in the 'O' shop (tool room), May 1931

After the First World War, female employees increasingly began to penetrate the traditionally male preserve of the GWR workshops. Here are two official views, in photogravure form, showing women at work in the laundry (above) and the polishing shop, *c*. 1920 (below)

'B' erecting and tender shop, east end, depicted in *c.* 1904 in another fine William Hooper postcard view

'A' machine and fitting shop: buffing connecting rods, 1949

'A' boiler shop: tapping fire-box stay-holes using hydraulic riveters

At work in a later era: changing the nameboard over the London Street Works entrance from 'British Railways Workshops' to 'British Rail Engineering Ltd', January 1970

'Trip'

His only pair

at

Trip

The Swindon Works Annual Holiday, the 'Trip' for the GWR workmen and their families was instituted in 1849. In later years the period of the 'Trip' was extended from a single day to a complete week, thus permitting the opportunity for a proper summer holiday for the workers of Swindon. Traditionally the 'Trip' period lasted from the first Friday in July until the following Monday week. Until 1938 the holiday was unpaid, when it was resumed after the Second World War the 'Trip' holiday was extended to two weeks with full pay.

In its Edwardian heyday, huge numbers departed from Swindon on 'Trip' morning. In 1905, nearly 25,000 people (approximately half the population) left Swindon in twenty-two special trains bound for resorts such as Weymouth, Weston and Torquay.

This postcard (left) was sent by Fred Strange, holidaying in Tenby in 1911, to his brother at 3 Tilleys Cottages, Stratton St Margaret. He writes, 'Dear brother, It rains pouring & only brought one suit. Just picture me, not half, Sunday morning. From Fred'

The Departure of the Great Mob.

Preparations: (left) the annual scrub for 'Dad' and best clothes for all the family were prerequisites of 'Trip'. Departure: (above) the large numbers travelling often resulted in an early morning start, crowded trains and great excitement. The lower postcard was actually sent from a Swindon lady to relations on holiday in Penzance in 1910, with the comment, 'Just a reminder of Friday morning!'

The holiday (above): come rain or shine, the holiday was enjoyed by most as a welcome respite from the drabness of workaday Swindon

The return (left and below): after the holiday, many families' finances were often in a parlous state, particularly as until 1913 no pay was drawn on the first pay-day after 'Trip'. This resulted in a 'grand march' past the empty tables. In 1913 the holiday was altered to mid-week dates so that half a week's pay could be drawn either side of the holiday

Trip activity to the west of Swindon station in 1906, photographed by William Hooper, with the carriage shops to the left and main Works offices to the right. Considering that this is the London to Bristol main line, the trippers appear to have scant regard for their own safety as they mill about the tracks

The same location as the previous photograph, outside the carriage shops, again photographed by Hooper, 1909. The engine is Dean-designed 2–4–0 No. 3208

GREAT WESTERN RAILWAY

SWINDON WORKS ANNUAL HOLIDAY.

THURSDAY & FRIDAY, JULY 6th & 7th, 1939.

Newquay, St. Ives & Penzance Trains

THESE TRAINS WILL START FROM
THE STATION, DOWN LINE PLATFORMS,
ON THURSDAY NIGHT, 6th JULY,
CALLING AT THE FOLLOWING STATIONS:—

		Train No. 1 Platform 4	Train No. 2 Platform 4	Train No. 6 Platform 4	Train No. 7 Platform 4 (Friday morning)
		P.M.	P.M.	A.M.	A.M.
SWINDON	dep.	9-0	10-5	12-25	12-50
Wootton Bassett	,,	9-10	10-15	12-35	1-3
Liskeard	arr.	—	—	—	6-25
Bodmin Road	,,	—	—	6-0	—
Lostwithiel	,,	—	—	6-8	—
Par	,,	—	—	6-20	—
NEWQUAY	,,	—	—	—	8-10
St. Austell	,,	—	—	6-33	—
Truro	,,	3-15 a.m.	4-20 a.m.	7-0	—
Perranwell	,,	—	4-50	—	—
Penryn	,,	—	5-2	—	—
Penmere	,,	—	5-9	—	—
FALMOUTH	,,	—	5-15	—	—
Truro	dep.	3-25	4-30	7-14	—
Redruth	arr.	—	4-50	—	—
Camborne	,,	—	5-2	—	—
Gwinear Rd.	,,	—	—	7-44	—
Hayle	,,	—	5-16	—	—
St. Erth	,,	4-5	5-23	—	—
Carbis Bay	,,	4-28	5-48	—	—
ST. IVES	,,	4-35	5-55	—	—
PENZANCE	,,	—	—	8-15	—

These trains are exclusively for passengers for Liskeard and stations beyond.

NOTE. Passengers for Plymouth, Devonport and Saltash must travel by the 5-15 a.m. train from Rodbourne Lane Sidings on Friday, July 7th.

Passengers for ST. IVES must travel by Train No. 1 or 2 as indicated on permit issued with ticket.

Passengers for REDRUTH, CAMBORNE, HAYLE and the FALMOUTH BRANCH must travel by Train No. 2. FALMOUTH passengers travel in through coaches which will be at the rear of the train.

Passengers for BODMIN (a), WADEBRIDGE (a), FOWEY (b), PAR, ST. AUSTELL, TRURO, PERRANPORTH (c), HELSTON (d) and PENZANCE must travel by Train No. 6.

Passengers for LISKEARD, LOOE (e) and NEWQUAY must travel by Train No. 7.

(a) Change at Bodmin Road.   (d) Change at Gwinear Road.
(b) Change at Lostwithiel.   (e) Change at Liskeard.
(c) Change at Truro.

Passengers for the branch line stations proceed, after leaving the special train, by the first ordinary train.

PRIVILEGE TICKETS DURING HOLIDAY PERIOD.

If Orders are required during the Holiday Period, application, giving full particulars, should be sent to the Manager's Office (Loco. or Carriage & Wagon, as the case may be), marked "Privilege Tickets," accompanied by a stamped addressed envelope. In the case of children, the age and sex must be given.

Trip handbill, 1939 (left). In this last peacetime summer approximately 27,000 people departed from Swindon in thirty special trains

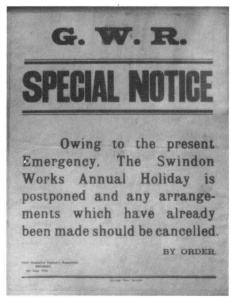

G. W. R.

SPECIAL NOTICE

Owing to the present Emergency, The Swindon Works Annual Holiday is postponed and any arrangements which have already been made should be cancelled.

BY ORDER.

Wartime emergencies led to the cancellation of 'Trip' from 1940 to 1945. This poster, issued at Swindon in June 1940, conveys the stark information

BRITISH RAILWAYS
(WESTERN REGION)
NOTICE
SWINDON WORKS
ANNUAL HOLIDAY, 1953

ARRANGEMENTS FOR TRAVEL

FORWARD JOURNEY.   Special Trains will be run as under :—

FRIDAY NIGHT, July 3rd.

Swindon dep. 9 55 p.m. for St. Ives - arr. 4 55 a.m.	Swindon dep. 11 52 p.m. for Birkenhead - arr. 5 10 a.m.
„ „ 10 30 „ for Newquay - „ 5 40 „	„ „ 11 45 „ for Penzance - „ 7 30 „
„ „ 11 15 „ for Blackpool - „ 5 53 „	

Passengers for Scotland travel Friday, July 3rd by 7 40 p.m. ordinary train Swindon to Paddington due 9 35 p.m. thence by ordinary services to destination via Euston or Kings Cross.

SATURDAY MORNING, July 4th.

Swindon dep. 6 0 a.m. for Torquay and Paignton arr. 9 52 a.m.	Swindon dep. 7 25 a.m. for Guildford.
„ „ 6 25 „ for Weymouth - „ 9 7 „	Three Bridges (connection to Bognor and Littlehampton).
„ „ 6 27 „ for Reading and Paddington „ 8 10 „	Brighton - arr. 11 15 a.m.
„ „ 6 47 „ for Weymouth - „ 9 38 „	and Eastbourne - „ 12 5 p.m.
„ „ 6 50 „ for Folkestone, Dover, Deal,	(connection at Eastbourne for Hastings)
Sandwich, Ramsgate,	Swindon dep. 7 47 a.m. for South Wales - Tenby arr. 1 20 p.m.
Broadstairs, Margate „ 1 0 p.m.	„ 7 55 „ for Exmouth „ 11 36 a.m.
„ „ 7 10 „ for Dawlish Warren, Dawlish,	and Minehead „ 11 20 „
Teignmouth, Torquay,	Swindon Town dep. 8 18 a.m. for Portsmouth and Southsea
Paignton „ 11 24 a.m.	and Portsmouth Harbour arr. 11 40 „
and Bideford - „ 12 20 p.m.	„ 9 55 „ for Southampton and
(connection at Barnstaple for Ilfracombe)	Bournemouth „ 1 22 p.m.
	Swindon dep. 10 45 a.m. for Weston-Super-Mare „ 12 25 „

Passengers for Clacton, Yarmouth, Skegness, etc., travel via London leaving Swindon by special train to Paddington as shewn above.

Passengers for Leicester, Nottingham, Sheffield, York, Scarborough, Filey, Bridlington, Newcastle, etc., travel by 11 5 a.m. train from Swindon via Banbury on Saturday, July 4th.

MONDAY, July 6th

Swindon dep. 7 52 a.m. for Weymouth arr. 10 17 a.m.	Swindon dep. 8 25 a.m. for Weston-Super-Mare arr. 10 7 a.m.
„ 8 10 „ for „ „ 11 0 „	„ „ 8 35 „ for Reading and Paddington „ 10 35 „

TUESDAY, July 7th

Swindon dep. 8 10 a.m. for Weymouth - arr. 11 0 a.m.	
„ „ 8 25 „ for Weston-Super-Mare „ 10 7 „	

Passengers on Monday and Tuesday, the 6th and 7th July, for destinations not covered by the above special trains, may travel by ordinary trains.

SUNDAY, 5th July.   Passengers may travel by ordinary trains.

WEDNESDAY, 8th July to SATURDAY, 18th July inclusive.   Employees who have intimated their intention on their application forms to make the forward journey on any of these dates will be permitted to travel by ordinary services except that on Saturday, 11th July, a special service is being run for West of England passengers as under :-

SATURDAY, 11th July.   Swindon, dep. 6-25 a.m. for West of England (Paignton arr. 10-35 a.m.)

The above times are subject to possible minor alteration and detailed information will be shewn on the time tables to be issued later.

RETURN JOURNEY.

SUNDAY, 5th July.   Passengers may return by ordinary trains.

MONDAY, 6th July.   Special trains will be run during the evening of each of these days from Weston-super-Mare and Weymouth giving a satisfactory day trip.
TUESDAY, 7th July.   Employees returning on these dates from stations not covered by these specials may travel by ordinary services.

WEDNESDAY, 8th July, THURSDAY, 9th July, FRIDAY, 10th July.   Passengers may return by ordinary trains.

SATURDAY, 11th July.   Special trains will be run covering practically all stations on this date giving an arrival at Swindon during the evening.   Passengers from stations not covered by the special trains will be permitted to travel by ordinary services.

SUNDAY, 12th July to FRIDAY, 17th July, inclusive.   Passengers may return by ordinary trains.

SATURDAY, 18th July.   Special trains will be run covering practically all stations on this date giving an arrival at Swindon during the evening.   Passengers from stations not covered by the special trains will be permitted to travel by ordinary services.

SUNDAY, 19th July.   Employees who have indicated on their application forms their intention to return on this date may travel by ordinary services.

NOTE.   It should be understood that employees travelling by ordinary trains to or from destinations which are covered by the special trains on the dates when the latter are run, will be required to pay the full ordinary fare.

PASSENGERS FOR IRELAND.

Services are available from Fishguard to Rosslare and also from Fishguard to Waterford and Works Holiday free tickets will be made out to either destination in accordance with applications.   The boats sail outwards each week-night to Rosslare and on Monday, Wednesday and Friday nights to Waterford.

During the period of the Swindon Works Holiday, "SAILING TICKETS" will be required for outwards journeys on the nights of July 3rd, 10th, 17th and 18th. Application for sailing tickets must be made as under :--

for outward journey to :-The Irish Traffic Superintendent, Central Enquiry Bureau, Bishops Bridge Road, PADDINGTON STATION, LONDON, W.2.
Sailing Tickets **not required** for return journeys during period of Works Holiday.

Applications for sailing tickets must be accompanied by a stamped addressed envelope and state clearly the proposed date of travel (together with an alternative date) and must indicate that applicant is a free ticket holder.

Mechanical & Electrical, and Carriage & Wagon Engineers' Departments,
SWINDON. June, 1953.

R. A. SMEDDLE,
C .T. ROBERTS.

Twitcher & Co. Ltd., Printers, Swindon.

SWINDON WORKS ANNUAL HOLIDAY 1953

Local Services in connection with the Works Holiday Specials will run as under:

WOOTTON BASSETT

		Friday, July 3rd		Saturday, July 4th		Monday, July 6th	Tuesday, July 7th A.M.	Saturday, July 11th P.M.	Saturday, July 18th P.M.
Swindon Junction	dep.					•	12- 5	11-0	9-53
Wootton Bassett	arr.						12-14	11-10	10-03
		P.M.	P.M.	A.M.	A.M.	A.M.			
Wootton Bassett	dep.	10-44	11-32	5-45	8-20	8-20			
Swindon Junction	arr.	10-53	11-40	5-54	8-30	8-30			

PURTON

		Friday, July 3rd		Saturday, July 4th		Monday, July 6th	Tuesday, July 7th	Saturday, July 11th			Saturday, July 18th			
						P.M.		P.M.	P.M.	P.M.	P.M.	P.M.	P.M.	P.M.
Swindon Junction	dep.					11-03		5-52	8-35	10-0	5-52	8-35	10-0	10-30
Purton	arr.					11-11		6-0	8-45	10-8	6-0	8-45	10-8	10-40
		P.M.	P.M.	A.M.	A.M.	A.M.	A.M.							
Purton	dep.	8-48	10-52	6-5	8-30	7-12	7-12							
Swindon Junction	arr.	8-58	11-0	6-13	8-38	7-20	7-20							

STRATTON and HIGHWORTH

					Monday, July 6th BUS P.M.	Tuesday, July 7th BUS	Saturday, July 11th BUS
Swindon Junction	dep.				10-55 B	10-45 B	11-00 B
Stratton	arr.				11-12 B	11-02 B	11-17 B
			A.M.	A.M.	A.M.		
Highworth	dep.		5-50	6-47	6-47		
Hannington	,,		5-55	6-52	6-52		
Stanton	,,		6-3	7-0	7-0		
Stratton	,,		6-8	7-6	7-6		
Swindon Junction	arr.		6-17	7-14	7-14		

B—Bristol Tramway Co. service, Junction Station to Stratton Park (X Rds.) via Kingsdown (X Rds.) and Lower Stratton Schools.

CHISELDON

					Monday, July 6th	Tuesday, July 7th	Saturday, July 11th P.M.	P.M.	Saturday, July 18th P.M.	P.M.
Swindon Junction	dep.						6-0	6-57	6-0	6-57
Swindon Town	,,						6-10	7-07	6-9	7-07
Chiseldon	arr.									
			P.M.	A.M.	A.M.	A.M.				
Chiseldon	dep.		8-26	9-05	6-57	6-57				
Swindon Town	arr.		8-35	9-13	7-5	7-5				
Swindon Junction	,,		——	——	9-32 7-5...					

		Chiseldon dep.	Swindon Town arr.	Swindon Junction
	P.M.	A.M.	A.M.	A.M.
Chiseldon	8-26	9-05	6-57	6-57
Swindon Town	8-35	9-13	9-32 / 7-5	7-5
Swindon Junction			9-40 / 7-15	7-15

SHRIVENHAM

					Monday, July 6th	Tuesday, July 7th	Saturday, July 11th P.M.	P.M.	Saturday, July 18th P.M.	P.M.
Swindon Junction	dep.				•	•	5-22	8-10	5-22	8-10
Stratton Park Halt	arr.						5-26	8-13	5-26	8-13
Shrivenham	,,						5-35	8-20	5-35	8-20
		P.M.	P.M.	A.M.	A.M.	A.M.				
Shrivenham	dep.	8-33	9-54	8-35	7-0	7-0				
Stratton Park Halt	,,	8-40	10-1	8-42	7-7	7-7				
Swindon Junction	arr.	8-45	10-6	8-48	7-17	7-17				

Note: Compartments for Passengers joining at Wootton Bassett will be reserved on Special Trains

No. 1	St. Ives	July 3rd
No. 405	Penzance	July 3rd
No. 8	Weymouth	July 4th
No. 9	Torquay Line	July 4th
No. 18	Weymouth	July 6th

THE WORKMEN'S TRAINS
Will run throughout the Holidays, (Mondays to Fridays) July 6th to 17th inclusive.

With the formation of British Railways in 1948, the responsibility for the organization of the annual Works holiday passed from the Mechanics' Institute to the Staff Office at Swindon Works. However, in practical terms, the 'Trip' arrangements remained much as they had been in GWR days, and the 1953 posters certainly retain a distinct GWR flavour

Extracts from the 1953 Special Arrangements booklet, which gave some idea of the operating difficulties involved. A total of twenty-three special trains carrying 15,800 passengers were scheduled to leave Swindon over a five-day period, with coaching stock being summoned from Plymouth, Bristol and Birmingham, and loaded trains departing from the loco yard and Rodbourne Lane due to pressure on space at Swindon station. Note the through trains on Friday night from Purton to Blackpool and from Wootton Bassett to Birkenhead

SUMMARY OF SPECIAL TRAINS.

No. of Special Train.	Departure Time from Swindon.	Train to start from	Destination	Train to be formed at	Empty Coaches arriving Swindon.	Thirds	Brake Thirds
FRIDAY NIGHT, 3rd JULY.							
	p.m.						
1	9.55	Down Main Platform	St. Ives	Tavistock Jct.	5† 36 p.m.	7	2
2	10.30	Down Main Platform	Newquay	Swindon Jct.	—	8	2
3	11.15	Up Main Platform	Blackpool	Cheltenham	11¶0 p.m.	9	2
40S	11.45	Down Main Platform	Bristol (for Penzance).	Exminster	7† 7 p.m.	11 and Compo	1 and Brake Compo
4	11.52	Up Main Platform	Birkenhead	Wootton Bassett	11Z40p.m.	7	2
SATURDAY, 4th JULY.							
	a.m.						
5	6. 0	Rodbourne Lane (Down Sidings).	Torquay and Paignton.	Swindon Jct.	—	11	2
6	6.25	Down Main Platform	Weymouth	Trowbridge	4†25 a.m.	9	2
7	6.27	Up Main Platform	Paddington	Swindon Jct.	—	13	2
8	6.47	Down Branch Platform	Weymouth	Westbury	5†25 a.m.	9	2
9	7.10	Rodbourne Lane (Down Sidings).	Paignton and Bideford.	Swindon Jct.	—	10	3 and Brake Compo
10	7.20	Up Main Platform	Eastbourne via Reading.	By S.R.	—	8	2
11	7.32	Up Main Platform	Margate via Reading.	Swindon Jct.	—	9	2
12	7.47	Down Main Platform	Tenby	Swindon Jct.	—	8	2
13	7.55	Rodbourne Lane (Down Sidings).	Exmouth and Minehead.	Swindon Jct.	—	10	3
14	8.18	Swindon Town	Portsmouth Hbr.	By S.R.	—	9	2
15	9.45	Swindon Town	Bournemouth (C.)	By S.R.	8†43 a.m.	6	2
16	10.45	Down Branch Platform	Weston-s-Mare	Marsh Pond	9†50 a.m.	8	2
MONDAY, 6th JULY.							
17	7.52	Down Main Platform	Weymouth	Swindon Jct.	—	11	2
18	8.10	Down Main Platform	Weymouth	Swindon Jct.	—	9	2
19	8.25	Down Branch Platform	Weston-s-Mare	Swindon Jct.	—	9	2
20	8.35	Up Main Platform	Paddington	Swindon Jct.	—	5	2
TUESDAY, 7th JULY.							
	a.m.						
21	8.10	Down Main Platform	Weymouth	Swindon Jct.	—	11	2
22	8.25	Down Main Platform	Weston-s-Mare	Swindon Jct.	—	9	2
SATURDAY, 11th JULY.							
	a.m.						
42S	6.25	Down Main Platform	Paignton	Swindon Jct.	—	9 and Compo	1 and Brake Compo

¶—Loaded train starts from Purton.   Z—Loaded train starts from Wootton Bassett.

NOTES.

Swindon Works will be closed at 5.20 p.m. on Friday, 3rd July, and will be re-opened at 7.40 a.m. on Monday, 20th July.

Passengers holding free tickets issued in connection with the Swindon Works Annual Holiday will not be allowed to travel by Ordinary Trains on the Forward or Return journeys on the dates on which Special Trains run except to and from the Stations not served by the Special Trains, in which cases they must travel by the Special Trains on the forward journey to join the Ordinary Trains at the point nearest the destination, and vice versa.

The free tickets will be stamped thus—S in the top right corner and will be dated 18th July except for those employees who have intimated their intention to return on 19th July, in which cases the tickets will be dated accordingly.

The Station Master, Swindon Junction, will have a record kept of the number of Passengers who alight on the return journey from Ordinary Trains, by counting the Tickets given up by the passengers. Each train and date to be kept separate.

Permits will be issued by the Mechanical and Electrical Engineer, and the Carriage and Wagon Engineer to enable relatives and friends of employees who are not entitled to free or privilege tickets to travel on the Special Trains with ordinary tickets. Such tickets will be obtainable at Swindon Junction Booking Office.

Guards working all forward and return trains are required to show on their journals a reliable estimate of the number of passengers conveyed and to render complete copies of LOCAL and THROUGH journals, shewing throughout times, to the Operating Superintendent.

Station-Masters at starting points of return trains to arrange for both sides of the front and rear vehicles, to be paper labelled " SWINDON."

BRITISH RAILWAYS (Western Region)

SWINDON WORKS ANNUAL HOLIDAY, 1953

WEYMOUTH TRAINS

SPECIAL TRAINS WILL RUN AS SHEWN BELOW:—

Starting from the Station Down Line Platform.

			Saturday July 4th		Monday, July 6th		Tuesday July 7th
		Train No. 6	8	17	18	21
		Platform No. 4	1	4	4	4
		A.M.	A.M.	A.M.	A.M.	A.M.
SWINDON	dep.	6.25	—	7.52	8.10	8.10
Wootton Bassett	"	—	6.58	—	8.21	8.21
Yeovil P.M.	arr.	—	8.32	9.25	9.59	9.59
Maiden Newton	"	—	9.09	—	10.30	10.30
Dorchester	"	—	9.20	—	10.42	—
WEYMOUTH	"	9.07	9.38	10.17	11.00	11.00

Passengers for LYME REGIS change at YEOVIL PEN MILL and proceed via YEOVIL TOWN.

Passengers for BRIDPORT change at MAIDEN NEWTON proceeding by ordinary train.

On Saturday, July 11th, passengers travel by 7.35 a.m. ordinary train from Swindon changing at Chippenham and Westbury proceeding thence 9.27 a.m. due Weymouth at 11.24 a.m.

On Sunday, July 5th,   } passengers may
" Wednesday, Thursday or Friday, July 8th, 9th or 10th   } travel by any
" any day, Sunday, July 12th to Friday, July 17th   } ordinary train.

Passengers for the Channel Islands travel on Monday, July 6th, by Special Train No. 18 as above, proceeding by Steamer from WEYMOUTH QUAY at 1.0 p.m.

PRIVILEGE TICKETS DURING HOLIDAY PERIOD.

If orders are required during the Holiday Period, application, giving full particulars, should be sent to the Manager's Office (Loco. or Carriage & Wagon, as the case may be) marked "Privilege Tickets," accompanied by a stamped addressed envelope. In the case of children, the age and sex must be given.

RETURN ARRANGEMENTS.

Passengers must return as shewn below; those from intermediate or branch line stations must connect with the train shewn at the nearest point.

		Monday July 6th		Tuesday July 7th	Saturday July 11th	Saturday July 18th
		Train No. 17	18	21	36	43
		P.M.	P.M.	P.M.	P.M.	P.M.
WEYMOUTH	dep.	7.10	7.55	7.10	1.55	1.55
Dorchester	"	—	8.17	—	—	—
Maiden Newton	"	—	—	—	2.34	2.34
Yeovil P. Mill	"	8.14	8.55	8.14	3.00	3.00
Wootton Bassett	arr.	—	10.35	10.02	4.50	4.50
SWINDON	"	10.10	10.47	10.10	5.01	5.01

On Sundays, July 5th, 12th and 19th   } passengers may return
" Wednesday, Thursday and Friday, July 8th, 9th and 10th   } by any
" any day, Monday to Friday, July 13th to 17th inclusive   } ordinary train.

Passengers may return from the Channel Islands on any date up to July 18th by the boat leaving Jersey 8.30 a.m. and Guernsey 10.45 a.m. and proceed from Weymouth to Swindon as under:—

On Saturdays, July 11th or 18th—by the 4.5 p.m. ordinary train from Weymouth Quay due Swindon 7.13 p.m.

On other days—by 3.40 p.m. from Weymouth Quay, changing at Frome and Westbury.

Passengers may also return by the additional service from the Islands on Saturday nights—Jersey dep. 7.45 p.m., Guernsey dep. 10.15 p.m.—proceeding by 6.5 a.m. from Weymouth Quay, Sunday mornings, due Swindon 10.15 a.m. (changing at Westbu.y).

The regulations in regard to SAILING TICKETS if return journey is made on a Saturday must be observed.

Free tickets are not available on the steamers on Saturdays but single privilege tickets are specially authorised for the return journey only.

Passengers travelling by any Trains other than those specified hereon will be required to pay the full Ordinary Fare.

Mech. and Elec., and Carr. and Wagon Engrs. Depts.,   R. A. SMEDDLE
Swindon.   C. T. ROBERTS
June, 1953

TWO

BOROUGH PRESS, SWINDON.

Weymouth trains, 'Trip' 1953. Five special trains carried 2,537 passengers to this popular seaside destination

The Medical Fund

The GWR established the Medical Fund Society in 1847 in order to provide welfare services to its employees and their families in Swindon by means of a mandatory subscription deducted from the wages of all men employed at Swindon Works. The Medical Fund served Swindonians 'from the cradle to the grave' for over one hundred years.

Two views of the Medical Fund Hospital in Faringdon Road, opened in 1872, showing medical staff and patients outside the main entrance. The upper photograph is a William Hooper postcard and shows the hospital decked for a royal occasion (probably the coronation of King George V in 1911)

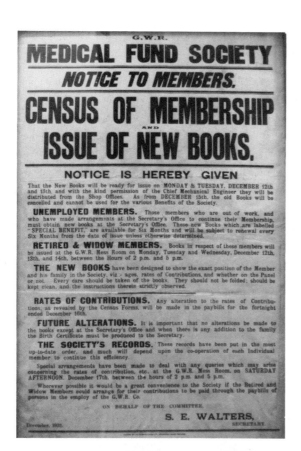

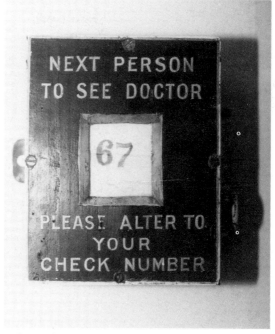

Left: Medical Fund Society notice, 1932. Above: a relic from the Medical Fund's consulting rooms, now preserved at Swindon Railway Museum. These devices were installed outside each doctor's surgery and remained in use until the 1980s

Another Edwardian view of the main hospital entrance

In 1892 a large red-brick building was erected by the Medical Fund Society at the corner of Milton Road and Faringdon Road to house new consulting rooms, a dispensary and swimming baths. An extension was built southwards along Milton Road in 1899 (above) to house washing, Turkish and Russian baths

The large swimming baths, looking towards the Faringdon Road end of the building. Note the changing cubicles alongside the pool, also the ornate wrought iron balcony and arched roof. When not required for swimming purposes, the baths could be boarded over and used as meeting rooms or dance floors

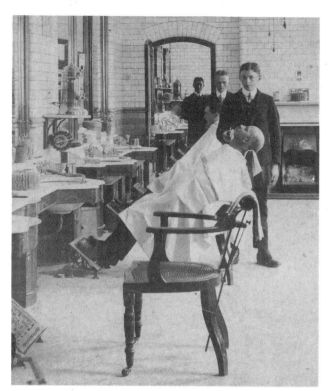

A hairdressing, shaving and shampooing salon (left) was also provided in the extended building for the use of both men and women

Dispensary waiting room (below). A Medical Fund Society notice on the wall to the left dates this photograph as 1909

The dispensary itself was situated within a secure walled area (above) and medicines dispensed to the public through small windows such as the one by which the gentleman in plus-fours is standing. On the other side of the wall (below), privacy was afforded by wooden screens and strict segregation of the sexes. This official GWR view dates from 1920 and shows doctors' surgeries to the left and the secretary's office in the background

The Broad Gauge Era

Two broad gauge 2–4–0 engines. Above: *Telford* of Sir Daniel Gooch's 'Victoria' class, built at Swindon in April 1863 and withdrawn in February 1879. Below: the huge No. 16, a convertible locomotive designed by William Dean which entered service, with its sister No. 18, in 1888. Built for the purpose of hauling the heavy 3 p.m. West of England express from Bristol as far as Swindon, these two engines were the most powerful express locomotives then running on the GWR

Another 2–4–0 design, *Hackworth* was one of the 'Hawthorn' or 'Avonside' class engines constructed by the Avonside Engine Company of Bristol for passenger work. This particular engine was built in May 1865 and withdrawn with the end of the broad gauge in 1892. *Hackworth* was one of twenty engines built at Bristol (a further six were erected at Swindon by the GWR) to a design by Sir Daniel Gooch, the specifications for which are reproduced opposite. Some of the particulars are quite precise, such as cylinders 'to be a mixture of best Shropshire cold blast and Blenavon iron'; boiler and fire-box 'to be covered with Cow Hair Felt and dry, well-seasoned Pine'; buffer-beam 'to be of sound Oak, with two Leather Buffers stuffed with Cork and Horse Hair'. Note also the livery of that period: green boiler and wheels, with brown frame picked out in red and black

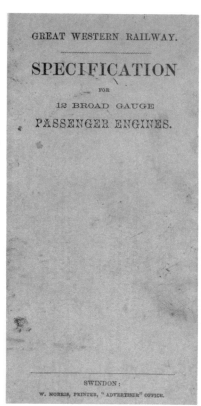

GREAT WESTERN RAILWAY.

SPECIFICATION

FOR

12 BROAD GAUGE

PASSENGER ENGINES.

SWINDON:

W. MORRIS, PRINTER, "ADVERTISER" OFFICE.

GREAT WESTERN RAILWAY.

Specification for Twelve Broad-Gauge Passenger Engines.

BOILER AND FIRE-BOX.

The Boiler Barrel to be of Low Moor, or other approved plates, with Baffle plates, &c., as per Drawing. Outside Fire-box to be of best Low Moor, or other approved plates. Inside Fire-box to be of Copper, with 186 Brass Tubes, two inches diameter. Sides and crown of Fire-box to be made of one plate. 1in. Copper stays, 9 crown stays, 7 longitudinal stays, Corner stays, and brick arch, as per Drawing.

FIRE BARS.

The Fire-bars to be of Wrought Iron to section, with Cast Iron toothed rack, as per Drawing.

SMOKE BOX.

The Tube plate to be of Low Moor, or other approved plates, tapered to cylindrical part of Boiler by Sin angle iron ring bored and faced. Top, sides, and front, to be of best Staffordshire plates, five-sixteenths of an inch thick. Door and inner door to be three-sixteenths of an inch thick, best Staffordshire plates.

CHIMNEY.

To be of best Staffordshire plates, ¼in. thick, with bell mouthed base, ¼-tenths in. thick, and Copper cap, as per Drawing.

FRAMES.

To be of Thorneycroft's best Staffordshire or Rotherham plate. Rubbing cheeks all to be of Wrought Iron, or Cast Steel.

WHEELS.

To be of Wrought Iron, with "Ince Forge" Steeled Tires, to section. Wheels to be forced on by hydraulic power, and crank pins to be case hardened. The Tires to be secured by "Gibson's" patent method, (see Drawing). The key iron required for this will be supplied by the Great Western Railway Company.

AXLES.

To be of best selected Scrap Iron. All straight Axle bearings to be case hardened.

AXLE-BOXES.

To be of Cast Iron, with Brass steps, and White Metal lining, and Cast Iron Grease boxes, with Wrought Iron cover, and leather lid sliding on spring pin.

SPRINGS.

All Pins to be turned, and the eyes and sockets bored. All Springs to be provided with auxiliary India-rubber pads in Cast iron case, as per Drawing.

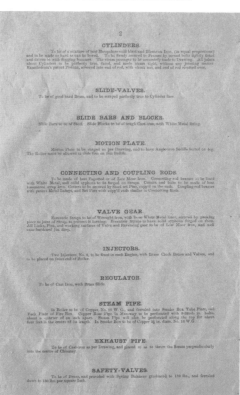

2

CYLINDERS.

To be of a mixture of best Shropshire cold blast and Blaenavon Iron, (in equal proportions) and to be made as hard as can be bored. To be firmly secured to Frames by turned bolts tightly fitted and driven in with flogging hammer. The steam passages to be accurately made to Drawing. All joints about Cylinders to be perfectly true, faced, and made steam tight, without any jointing matter. Ramsbottom's patent Piston, screwed into end of rod, with check nut, and end of rod rivetted over.

SLIDE-VALVES.

To be of good hard Brass, and to be scraped perfectly true to Cylinder face.

SLIDE BARS AND BLOCKS.

Slide Bars to be of Steel. Slide Blocks to be of tough Cast-iron, with White Metal facing.

MOTION PLATE.

Motion Plate to be shaped as per Drawing, and to have Angle-iron Saddle bolted on top. The Boiler must be allowed to slide free on this Saddle.

CONNECTING AND COUPLING RODS.

To be made of best Fagotted or of Low Moor Iron. Connecting-rod brasses to be lined with White Metal, and solid syphons to be forged on Straps. Cotters and bolts to be made of best hammered scrap Iron. Cotters to be secured by Steel set Pins, rivetted on the ends. Coupling-rod brasses with patent Metal linings, and Set Pins with syphon ends similar to Connecting Rods.

VALVE GEAR.

Eccentric Straps to be of Wrought Iron, with brass White Metal liner, secured by pinching piece at joint of Strap, to prevent it turning. Eccentric Straps to have solid syphons forged on them. All Links, Pins, and working surfaces of Valve and Reversing gear to be of Low Moor Iron, and well case-hardened ⅛in. deep.

INJECTORS.

Two Injectors, No. 8, to be fixed in each Engine, with Brass Clack Boxes and Valves, and to be placed on front end of Boiler.

REGULATOR.

To be of Cast Iron, with Brass Slide.

STEAM PIPE.

In Boiler to be of Copper, No. 10 W.G., and forended into Smoke Box Tube Plate, and Back Plate of Fire Box. Copper Rose Pipe in Man-way to be perforated with holes in halves, about a quarter of an inch apart. Steam Pipe will also be perforated along the top for about four feet in the centre of its length. In Smoke Box to be of Copper 3½ in. diam. No. 10 W.G.

EXHAUST PIPE.

To be of Cast-iron as per Drawing, and placed so as to throw the Steam perpendicularly into the centre of Chimney.

SAFETY-VALVES.

To be of Brass, and provided with Spring Balance graduated to 150 lbs., and ferruled down to 130 lbs. per square Inch.

3

PLATFORM, BUFFERS, &c.

Foot-plate and Platform along sides of Engine to be of plate Iron. Wrought-iron Tube Rail along sides of Boiler and in front of Fire-box. Buffer-beam to be of sound Oak, with two Leather Buffers stuffed with Cork and Horse Hair.

CLEADING.

Boiler and Fire-box to be covered with One Hair Felt, and with dry, well-seasoned Pine, battened to length of wood secured round. Boiler the thickness of the Felt, the whole to be covered with "Grecoid Plates," No. 13 Wire Gauge, glazed on the cover face, and secured with Wrought-iron Straps one-sixteenth of an inch thick, covering the joints of the plates. Suitable Copper Sheathing will also be required at back and front corners of Fire-box.

GENERAL FITTINGS.

All Glands and Working Parts to be provided with Syphons; Sand-box on each side of Engine near Driving Wheel with 1-inch Pipe to rail; 2 Whistles; 1 "Bourdon's" Pressure Gauge; a set of Spanners, with No. of Engine stamped on each. 2 Safety Valves in Brass Casing, and Steam Jet into Chimney to Drawing.

PAINTING.

Boilers to have four Coats Red Lead before Cleading. Cleading Plates to be painted two coats Red Lead inside. The Engine and Tender, when finished, to have four coats. The Boiler and Wheels to be Green, and the Frame Brown, picked out with Red and Black, — a sample of each Colour will be supplied to the Manufacturer.

TENDER.

WHEELS.

Six Wheels, Wrought-iron, with "Ince-Forge" Steeled Tires.

AXLE-BOXES.

Cast-iron, with Brass Journals lined with White Metal.

TANK.

To carry 1800 Gallons of Water; 1 Sand-box on Tender, with ¾-inch Pipe to Rail.

GENERAL STIPULATIONS.

The Manufacturer will be furnished with detail Drawings (which he must copy and return) of the various parts of the Engine and Tender.

All threads for Bolts and Nuts to be cut with "Whitworth's" Taps and Dies. "Rabbit's" Patent to be used wherever White Metal is mentioned. All Cast Iron to be of the best Shropshire Cold Blast or Blaenavon Pig. The Engine and Tender to be of the best Workmanship and Materials, and to be finished to the entire satisfaction of the Company's Engineer, and the Manufacturer must guarantee each Engine until it has run a distance of 1000 Miles, with average loads, on the Great Western Railway.

The Engines to be delivered in Working Order upon the Great Western Railway, as follows, viz:—3 in January, 3 in February, 3 in March, and 3 in April, 1865.

SWINDON, 12th August, 1864.

Two of Gooch's handsome 4–2–2 'Iron Duke' class, *Great Western* (above) and *Prometheus* (below). Both date from 1888 and, being non-convertible engines, were withdrawn and scrapped a mere four years later

Before and after conversion: No. 3024 in broad gauge form (above), and sister engine No. 3025 as adapted to narrow gauge (below) with wheels inside the frames. These engines were two of a batch of convertible six-wheelers built in 1891 as successors to the non-convertible 'Iron Duke' class

Distribution of Name-plates of Broad Gauge 8ft Engines.

Engine	Purchaser	Terms of Sale	Remarks
Alma	Mr C. Mortimer	6ᵈ per lb deld at Padd.	
Dᵒ		Dᵒ	
Amazon	Mr W. Garratt	£2/2/- deld at Swindon	
Dᵒ	Mr A. E. Mills	£6. deld at Swindon	Mounted in Mahogany with Coat of Arms &c
Balaklava	Rev A. H. Malan	1/- per lb deld at Swindon	
Dᵒ	Mechanics' Institution		
Bulkeley	Mr A. P. Heywood-Lonsdale		
Dᵒ	G.W.R. Board Room		
Courier	————	————	} Put to scrap
Dᵒ			3
Crimea	Mr H. Michel Whitley	£2/2/- deld at Swindon	
Dᵒ	Mr A. L. Radford	£2/2/- deld at Swindon	
Dragon	Mr H. Thomson Naish	£2/2/- deld at Swindon	
Dᵒ			
Emperor	Mr W. A. Robins	£2/2/- deld at Swindon	
Dᵒ			
Eupatoria	Mr R. H. Warren	£2/2/- deld at Swindon	
Dᵒ			
Great Britain	Mechanics' Institution		
Dᵒ	Railway Clearing House	Padd £40	
Inkermann	Mr A. Evans	£2/2/- deld at Swindon	
Dᵒ	Mr D. L. Evans	£2/2/- deld at Swindon	
Iron Duke	Rev A. H. Malan	1/- per lb deld at Swindon	
Dᵒ	Mechanics' Institution		
Lightning	Dᵒ		
Dᵒ	Railway Clearing House		
Prometheus	Mr C. Foxwell	7/6 per lb deld at Swindon	
Dᵒ	Mr R. Bensley	£2/2/- deld at Swindon	
Rover	Mr C. Mortimer	6ᵈ lb deld at Padd.	
Dᵒ		Dᵒ	
Sebastopol			
Dᵒ			
Sultan	Mr J. L. Wilkinson	Padd.	Mounted on Fire Screen
Dᵒ			
Swallow			
Dᵒ			
Tartar	Mr W. A. Robins	£2/2/- deld at Swindon	
Dᵒ			
Timour	Mr D. L. Evans	£2/2/- deld at Swindon	
Dᵒ			
Warlock	Rev A. H. Malan	1/- per lb deld at Swindon	
Dᵒ	Mr H. Thomson Naish	£2/2/- deld at Swindon	
Great Western	Mr A. P. Heywood-Lonsdale		
Dᵒ	G.W.R. Board Room		
Tornado	Rev A. H. Malan	1/- per lb deld at Swindon	
Dᵒ	Mr H. Thomson Naish	£2/2/- delivered at Swindon	

This 1892 manuscript list relates to the disposal of name-plates from the survivors of the broad gauge 'Iron Duke' class engines. These elegant Gooch-designed machines were originally built at Swindon between 1847 and 1850, and were later replaced by new engines bearing the original names between 1871 and 1888. The twenty-three engines on the list were all non-convertibles, and finished their active life with the demise of the broad gauge in 1892. All were put to scrap at Swindon. *Tornado*, the last broad gauge locomotive built at Swindon in 1888, had a working life of just under four years.

As can be seen, certain plates were retained by the GWR for display at Swindon and Paddington; others were offered for sale to employees, members of the Board of Directors and private purchasers, or consigned to the scrap-heap. Eight of the name-plates are now preserved at the GWR Museum, but the whereabouts of the others is uncertain. Missing from the list are the name-plates from *Hirondelle*, which was withdrawn two years earlier in 1890, and *Estafette*, scrapped in 1884.

A separate contemporary list shows that name-plates from 'Hawthorn' class engines *Blenkinsop*, *Dewrance*, *Melling* and *Murdock* were also awaiting disposal from the Loco factory in 1894. Some of the 'Iron Duke' plates were mounted for display purposes by the Carriage Department prior to disposal, notably *Amazon*, *Great Western*, *Lightning* and *Sultan*, the responsibility for this resting with G.J. Churchward, at that time Carriage Works Manager

Amazon, built at Swindon in 1878, and shown here in an official Works photograph *c.* 1890 in run-down condition

Carriage works cost sheet for mounting name-plate, 1893 (left), with *per pro* Churchward signature

Correspondence between Churchward and William Dean (below) relating to the *Great Western* name-plate

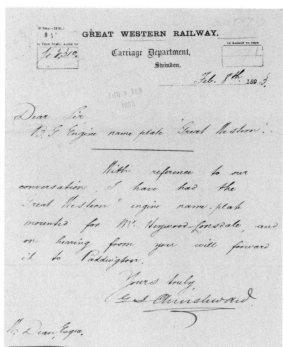

BROAD GAUGE LOC

(3128).

PASSENGER

"WOLF" CLASS. 15-in. CYLINDERS. ("STAR" CLASS. 16-in. CYLINDERS.)	BOGIE CLASS. 17-in. CYLINDERS.	METROPOLITAN TANK CLASS. 16-in. CYLINDERS.	"PRIAM" CLASS. 16-in. CYLINDERS.		"ALMA" CLASS. 18-in. CYLINDERS.	"ABBOT" CLASS. 17-in. CYLINDERS.
TANK ENGINES.			**ENGINES REQUIRING TENDERS.**			
Aeolus	Brigand	N.B.—These are in course of alteration to TENDER Engines May, 1869).	Achilles	Pluto	Alma	Abbot
Antelope	Corsair		Actæon	Priam	Amazon	Antiquary
Apollo	Euripides		Arab	Prince	Balaklava	Cœur-de-Lion
Assagais	Hesiod		Argus	Proserpine	Courier	Ivanhoe
Atlas	Homer		Arrow	Queen	Crimea	Lalla Rookh
Aurora	Horace	Bee	Bellona	Royal Star	Dragon	Pirate
Bright Star	Juvenal	Bey	Castor	Saturn	Emperor	Red Gauntlet
Comet	Lucan	Camelia	Centaur	Spitfire	Estaffete	Robin Hood
Creese	Lucretius	Czar	Charon	Stag	Eupatoria	Rob-Roy
Djerid	Ovid	Fleur-de-lis	Cyclops	Stentor	Great Britain	Waverley
Eagle	Sappho	Gnat	Demon	Sylph	Great Western	
Eclipse	Seneca	Kaiser	Dart	Tiger	Hirondelle	
Fire-Ball	Statius	Khan	Dog-Star	Venus (No. 2.)	Inkermann	
Fire-King	Theocritus	Locust	Electra	Vesta	Iron Duke	
Gazelle	Virgil	Mosquito	Elk	Vulture	Kertch	
Giraffe	No. 1 (V. N.)	Rose	Erebus	Western Star	Lightning	
Hesperus	„ 2 „	Shah	Evening Star	Wild-fire	Lord of the Isles	
Javelin	„ 3 „	Shamrock	Falcon	Witch	Pasha	
Lance	„ 4 „	Thistle	Fire-brand		Perseus	
Meridian	„ 5 „	Wasp	Fire-Fly		Prometheus	
Meteor	„ 6 „		Ganymede		Rougemont	
North Star			Gorgon		Rover	
Orion			Greyhound		Sebastopol	
Polar Star			Harpy		Sultan	"VICTORIA" CLASS. 16-in. CYLINDERS.
Red Star			Hecate		Swallow	
Rising Star			Hector		Tartar	
Rocket			Hydra		Timour	
Shooting Star			Ixion		Tornado	
Snake			Jupiter	METROPOLITAN TENDER CLASS. 16-in CYLINDERS.	Warlock	Abdul Medjid
Stiletto			Leopard		Wizard	Alexander
Sun			Lethe			Brindley
Sunbeam			Load Star			Brunel
Venus (No. 1.)			Lucifer			Fulton
Viper			Lynx	Azalia		Leopold
Vulcan			Mars	Hornet		Locke
Wolf			Mazeppa	Laurel		Napoleon
Yataghan			Medea	Lily		Oscar
Zebra			Medusa	Mogul		Otho
			Mentor	Myrtle		Rennie
			Mercury	Violet		Smeaton
			Milo			Stephenson
			Minos			Telford
			Morning Star			Trevethick
			Panther			Victor Emanuel
			Pegasus			Victoria
			Peri			Watt
			Phœnix			

The Swindon list of engines, c. 1870. Note that all the Great Western broad gauge non-convertible engines had names but no numbers. The proliferation of classical names intrigued the railway historian, E. T. MacDermot, who wrote that they 'smacked largely of having been forcibly extracted from a dictionary of Greek and Roman

OMOTIVE ENGINES.

GOODS

TANK ENGINES.

ENGINES REQUIRING TENDERS.

HAWTHORN CLASS. 16-in. CYLINDERS.	"LEO" CLASS. 15-in. CYLINDERS.	"FURY" CLASS. 16-in. CYLINDERS.	"CÆSAR" CLASS. 17-in. CYLINDERS.				"SWINDON" CLASS. 17-in. CYLINDERS.
° Altered from PRIAM Class.	Aquarius	Ajax	Alligator	Liffey	Tamar		Bath
	Aries	Argo	Amphion	Luna	Tantalus		Birmingham
Acheron °	Buffalo	Bacchus	Ariadne	Magi	Tay		Bristol
Avonside	Cancer	Bellerophon	Avon	Mammoth	Thames		Chester
Beyer	Capricornus	Bergion	Banshee	Mersey	Theseus		Gloucester
Blenkinsop	Dromedary	Briareus	Behemoth	Metis	Thunderer		Hereford
Bury	Elephant	Brontes	Boyne	Midas	Trafalgar		London
Cerberus °	Etna	Dreadnought	Brutus	Minerva	Tweed		Newport
Dewrance	Gemini	Fury	Cæsar	Monarch	Tyne		Oxford
Fenton	Hecla	Goliah	Caliban	Nelson	Typhon		Reading
Foster	Leo	Hercules	Caliph	Nemesis	Ulysses		Shrewsbury
Gooch	Libra	Jason	Cambyses	Neptune	Vesper		Swindon
Hackworth	Pisces	Premier	Cato	Nero	Vixen		Windsor
Hawk °	Sagittarius	Sampson	Ceres	Nimrod	Volcano		Wolverhampton
Hawthorn	Scorpio	Telica	Champion	Nora Creina	Warhawk		
Hedley	Stromboli	Tityos	Chronos	Octavia	Warrior		
John Gray	Taurus	Vesuvius	Cicero	Olympus	Wear		
Melling	Virgo		Clyde	Orpheus	Wellington		
Murdoch			Coquette	Orson	Wye		
Ostrich °	**"SIR WATKIN" CLASS.** 17-in. CYLINDERS.		Cossack	Osiris	Xerxes		
Peacock			Creon	Pallas	Zetes		
Penn	Bulkeley		Cupid	Pandora	Zina		
Phlegethon °	Fowler		Cyprus	Panthea			
Pollux °	Miles		Diana	Pearl			
Roberts	Saunders		Dido	Pelops			
Sharp	Sir Watkin	**VALE OF NEATH CLASS.** 18-in. CYLINDERS.	Druid	Pioneer			
Stewart	Whetham		Esk	Plutarch			
Wood	**BANKING CLASS.** 17-in. CYLINDERS.	No. 13	Ethon	Plutus			
	Avalanche	,, 14	Europa	Plym			
	Bithon	,, 15	Flirt	Psyche			
	Iago		Flora	Pyracmon			
	Juno		Florence	Regulus			
	Plato		Forth	Remus			
	VALE OF NEATH CLASS.		Geryon	Rhea			
			Giaour	Rhondda			
	No. 7 CYL. 17½		Gladiator	Romulus			
	,, 8 ,,		Gyfeillon	Ruby			
	,, 9 ,,		Hades	Salus			
	,, 10 17		Hebe	Severn			
	,, 11 ,,		Hecuba	Severus			
	,, 12 ,,		Hero	Shannon			
	,, 16 17½		Humber	Sibyl			
	,, 17 ,,		Iris	Sirius			
	,, 18 ,,		Janus	Sphinx			
	,, 19 ,,		Lagoon	Steropes			
			Leander	Sylla			
			Leonidas	Talbot			

antiquities.' Certainly names such as *Gnat*, *Witch*, *Gyfeillon*, *Yataghan* and *Flirt* do appear to be curious choices

GREAT WESTERN RAILWAY.

RULES AND REGULATIONS

TO BE OBSERVED BY

WORKMEN EMPLOYED IN THE WORKSHOPS

OF THE

LOCOMOTIVE, CARRIAGE AND WAGON DEPARTMENTS.

Condition of Service. · 1. Every applicant for employment must be in good health, and will only be temporarily engaged until a satisfactory character has been received from his last employer for whom he has worked six months. He must produce his Certificate of Birth, and must sign a declaration that he has read a copy of these Rules, and that he undertakes to observe and be bound by them as a condition of his employment.

Hours of work. 2. The usual hours of work are as follow :—

Monday to Friday { 6.0 a.m. to 8.15 a.m. / 9.0 ,, ,, 1. 0 p.m. / 2.0 p.m. ,, 5.30 p.m.

Saturdays ... { 6.0 a.m. to 8.15 a.m. / 9.0 ,, ,, 12. 0 noon

totalling 54 hours per week, or an average of nine hours per day.

Sick and Medical Fund Societies. 3. Every workman is required, as a condition of Service, to become a Member of the G.W.R. Medical Fund Society, for providing medicines and medical attendance for the members and their families, and a member of the G.W.R. Sick Fund Society, unless he is already in Benefit Societies

2

Overtime will be reckoned after 5.30 p.m. each day, except Saturday, when it will be reckoned after 12.0 noon. It will be valued at the rate of time and quarter up to 10.0 p.m., and time and half after that hour. This clause applies only to men who have worked the full number of hours during the day.

Men not regularly employed on Sunday duty will be paid for Sunday work at the rate of time and half.

No overtime will be allowed until 54 hours per week have been made, except when work is stopped by reason of accidents to machinery, or when a man has, under pressure of work, worked all the previous night, or when the works are closed at holiday times ; Sunday work to stand by itself.

Gas makers, Furnacemen, and others whose ordinary working hours do not correspond with this rule, will be paid according to arrangements made to suit the circumstances of each case.

3

which provide adequate sick benefit in case of sickness.

NOTE.—*This rule applies to Swindon Works only.*

Resignation and dismissal. 4. The engagement to be terminable by 9 working hours' notice on either side. In case of misconduct the workman will be liable to instant dismissal.

Absence from duty. 5. Any workman absent from the works more than ¼ day, whether from illness or otherwise, must notify the Foreman of the shop, stating the cause of absence.

Any workman absent from work for two days without leave, will be considered as having left the Service, as from the commencement of the absence.

Any workman absent from duty through lead poisoning, must at once inform his Foreman, so that the case may be reported to H.M. Factory Inspector.

Time tickets and time recorders. 6. Each workman will be provided with a number which will be stamped upon the metal ticket, or time recording card supplied. He must place the ticket in the box provided for the purpose each time he enters the works. Workmen who are required to record their time by Time Recorders must strictly observe the instructions laid down for the use of the machines.

4

Any workman having lost or mislaid his ticket, can have his time booked by reporting the matter to the ticket man before the box is closed, but a charge of 6d. will be made for a new ticket. Any workman being present at the commencement of a period of work, and failing to book his time, may have his time booked, provided he can, during the period of work, prove to the satisfaction of his Foreman that he was present at its commencement, and will be liable to a fine of 6d. Any workman putting in a ticket other than his own, or tampering with the Time Recorder, will be liable to instant dismissal.

Time books and time sheets. 7. Each workman must enter in the book or time sheet provided for the purpose, the name and description of the work on which he has been employed during the previous day, and if on more than one job, the time on each. Any workman neglecting to enter the time correctly, or to deposit the book or sheet at the proper time and place, will be liable to a fine of 6d.

Cash boxes. 8. The cash boxes in which the wages are paid must be deposited in the box provided for their collection before 9 o'clock on the Monday morning following the pay. Any workman neglecting to do this will be liable to a fine of 6d.

5

Quarrelling idling, &c. 9. Any workman found playing, idling or quarrelling during working hours will be liable to a fine of 2s. 6d., and, in the event of an accident occurring through such misconduct, the workman in default must pay any or all expenses to which the Company may be put.

Ceasing work before hooter sounds, and unauthorised washing. 10. Any workman leaving off work or washing without proper authority before the hooter sounds, or washing his hands in oil, will be liable to a fine of 1s. for each offence.

Leaving or entering works. 11. Any workman leaving or entering the premises by any way other than the doors appointed, will be liable to instant dismissal.

Leaving works during working hours, and taking out material. 12. Any workman leaving the works during working hours, without permission, will forfeit his wages from the commencement of that period of the day, and be liable to a fine of 1s. in addition. No one will be allowed at any time to take out of the works any tool or material unless authorized by a pass from his Foreman, which must state the number of the pieces. No workman, except those providing their own tools, is allowed to carry any basket or parcel into the works, but must leave it with the attendants in the Mess Room. All passes must be left with the gatekeeper, who is required to take account of material of any kind taken out of the works.

6

Tools. 13. Every workman will be held responsible for the tools entrusted to him, and he will be required to see that the initials of the Company, as well as his own private mark are upon them, or be liable to a fine of 1s.

Borrowing tools. 14. A workman borrowing tools from another must return them, and in the event of their being lost or damaged may be called upon to pay their value.

Personal tools to be insured. 15. Every workman must provide himself with such personal tools as are usual in his trade, and must insure them ; the Company will not be responsible for any such tools which may be destroyed or injured by fire.

Taps, dies, rimers, &c. 16. A workman using taps, dies, rimers, or other general tools, must see that they are returned in good condition to the person appointed to take charge of them, or he will be liable to a fine of 2s. 6d.

Unauthorised making of tools. 17. Any workman making a tool without instructions from his Foreman, will be liable to a fine of 2s. 6d., or to instant dismissal.

Lubricants and dirty waste. 18. For every drilling, planing, or nut cutting machine, the prescribed lubricant must be used.

7

A workman using oil without being specially ordered to do so by his Foreman, will be liable to a fine of 1s. Dirty or greasy waste must not be left lying about, but must be placed in the receptacle for such material.

Damage to machinery, &c. 19. A workman using a machine or other article improperly, or damaging it through neglect, shall pay the amount of the damage, and be liable to instant dismissal.

Use of improper material. 20. A workman making use of any material which is cracked or otherwise unfit for the purpose for which it is intended, will be liable to a fine of 2s. 6d., or to instant dismissal.

Inferior workmanship. 21. A workman making an article of wrong dimensions, or finishing work in an inferior or unworkmanlike manner, may be called upon to make good such work, and be liable to a fine of 2s. 6d., or to instant dismissal.

Handing in of keys before leaving service. 22. A workman leaving the service of the Company, will not be paid his wages until he delivers up the key of his drawer or tool chest, and the tools entrusted to him, to the satisfaction of the person authorized to receive them.

8

Smiths and Strikers not to fetch coal. 23. Smiths and Strikers will not be allowed to fetch in slack or coals to their fires, excepting where men are not specially appointed for that purpose.

Smiths to extinguish fires. 24. Where men are not specially appointed for the duty, Smiths are required to see that their fires are put out every night before leaving, and that the blast is shut off, or be liable to a fine of 2s. 6d.

Gas, lights, &c., to be extinguished. 25. Where men are not specially appointed for the duty, every workman must shut off the gas or put out the lights he has been using, before going to meals or leaving off work, or he will be liable to a fine of 1s.

Workmen not to enter shops other than their own. 26. A workman who goes into a workshop in which he is not usually employed, except by the order of his Foreman, will be liable to a fine of 2s. 6d.

Intoxicating liquor. 27. A workman who brings intoxicating liquor into the works will be liable to instant dismissal.

Smoking. 28. A workman who smokes in the workshops, or within the precincts of the works, will be liable to a fine of 2s. 6d.

9

Stores. 29. All Stores required must be obtained from the Storekeeper by an order signed by the Foreman of the shop. If any brass or other material is lost, the workman in charge of the same will be held responsible, and if no satisfactory account can be given, he will be liable to a fine of 2s. 6d., or to instant dismissal.

Breaking open drawers, boxes, &c. 30. A workman who breaks open another workman's drawer or box, or any box containing tools belonging to a lathe or other piece of machinery, will be liable to a fine of 2s. 6d., or to instant dismissal.

A workman who locks up any drill, brace, or other general tool, or tools belonging to any piece of machinery (unless he is working constantly at that machine), will be liable to a fine of 2s. 6d., or to instant dismissal.

Cleaning machinery. 31. The moving parts of any Engine, Crane, Lathe, or other machine, must not be oiled or cleaned while in motion. The legs, beds, and frames may be cleaned during the week, but the other parts on Saturdays only, when 15 minutes will be allowed for cleaning a single lathe or machine, and 20 minutes for a crank lathe, a double-headed lathe, or two machines. The parts of a lathe or machine must not be changed while

in motion. No workman must attempt to put on a strap or interfere with the main shafting in any way while the engine is in motion.

A workman who violates any provision of this rule will be considered *guilty of serious and wilful misconduct*, and to have rendered himself liable to instant dismissal.

Removing borings, drillings, turnings, &c., from machinery. 32. Sticks and brushes are provided for the purpose of removing drillings, turnings, etc., from the tools of machines, and any workman removing them with his fingers, will be considered *guilty of serious and wilful misconduct*, and render himself liable to instant dismissal.

Wearing of jackets. 33. It is *most* important that Workmen employed on lathes and other machines, should wear close fitting jackets.

Free tickets. 34. Any Workman travelling with a free ticket on this Company's line must give the same up to the Station-Master or Ticket Collector at the end of his journey. No Workman may ride upon an Engine without proper authority.

Privilege tickets. 35. The Company, in granting privilege ticket facilities, rely on the co-operation of all their Workmen to prevent abuse of the privilege, and to report any irregularity which may come under their notice.

11

Any Workman detected transferring an order or ticket issued, or being privy to such transfer, will be liable to instant dismissal and prosecution.

Disobedience and misconduct. 36. Any Workman guilty of disobedience to his superiors, or adjudged guilty of serious misconduct, will be liable to instant dismissal.

Trading. 37. No Workman is allowed to trade whilst in the Company's service.

Inability to attend pay table. 38. Any Workman not able to attend at the pay table, must use the prescribed form, countersigned by his Foreman, authorising someone to receive his money.

Definition of workman. 39. The term "Workman" in these Rules include "Women," and "Young Persons," as defined in the Factory and Workshops Act of 1901.

BY ORDER.

LOCO', CARRIAGE AND WAGON DEPT.,
ENGINEER'S OFFICE,
SWINDON,
1904.

I, the undersigned, having been appointed as *Frame Builder* in the service of the Great Western Railway Company, do hereby bind myself to observe and obey the foregoing Rules and Regulations; and hereby declare that I have carefully read them (or have had them read to me), and that I clearly understand them and have received a copy of the same.

As witness my hand this _1st_ day of _October_ 19 0 9.

Signature *C Dyke*

Witness to } *W Tock*
Signature }

The 1904 Rule Book for employees in the GWR workshops is reproduced here in full. Of especial note are the fifty-four hour working week; the various fines which could be imposed for relatively minor misdemeanours; and the compulsory membership of the Company's Medical and Sick Fund Societies for all employees

Great Western Railway.

Locomotive & Carriage Department.

ENGINEER'S OFFICE.

Swindon 28ᵗʰ March 1911.

Mr Edwin Thomas James Evans, who, I understand, is seeking an appointment as Locomotive Draughtsman on the New South Wales Government Railways, has applied to me for a testimonial as to his service under this Company.

I have pleasure in stating that Mr Evans entered our employ on the 6ᵗʰ January 1896 & on the 22ⁿᵈ of the following September was apprenticed to Engine Fitting & Turning for a term of six years. During his apprenticeship he was employed in our Fitting, Turning & Erecting Shops, Testing House & Drawing Office.

Upon the completion of his time he remained in my principal Drawing Office, where he has since been engaged on arrangement & detail design of locomotives & boilers.

He is a good draughtsman, has a thorough knowledge of locomotive engines & whilst in this Company's service has given us every satisfaction.

G. Churchward
*Chief Superintendent,
G.W.R. Loco, Carr, & Wagon Department.*

GREAT WESTERN RAILWAY.

LOCOMOTIVE, CARRIAGE & WAGON DEPARTMENT.
CHIEF MECHANICAL ENGINEER'S OFFICE.
Mʳ. SWINDON, WILTS.
(TRAIN G.W. 6).

Sat. 5th August 1922.

Your reference:

Telegraphic Address:
Loco, Swindon.

Telephone:
185, Swindon.

PRIVATE

Please quote this reference:—
E.
AJLW.

My dear Sir,

DEPARTMENTAL RE-ORGANISATION.

With reference to conversation, I write to confirm the intimation that the Directors at their meeting yesterday appointed you to the post of Carriage and Wagon Works Manager vice Mr R.A.G.Hannington, with an increase in salary from £550 to £750 per annum, to date from the 14th instant.

The post of Assistant Manager will be taken by Mr H.F.V.Dawson, at present Mechanical Inspector, Locomotive Works, with an increase in salary from £400 to £450 per annum. This appointment will also date from the 14th instant.

Yours faithfully,

C.B.Collett

E.T.J.Evans, Esq.,
SWINDON.

Ephemera of employment. Top left: a glowing reference from Churchward for Edwin Evans, 1911, who in fact decided to stay with the GWR and rose to the rank of Carriage & Wagon Works Manager, which position he held from 1922 (above) until his retirement in 1946. Bottom left: a character reference from 1909; note the Chief Superintendent's prestigious telegraphic address. Below: a curt Termination of Apprenticeship note, signed by R.A. Hannington, Locomotive Works Manager

---

Great Western Railway.

Locomotive, Carriage & Wagon Department.

ENGINEER'S OFFICE.

Swindon, Wilts,

April 27th. 1909.

H.

Telegraphic Address.
CHURCHWARD, SWINDON.

Nat. Telephone Nº 32, SWINDON.

IN REPLY

TO YOUR:-

IN YOUR REPLY

PLEASE QUOTE:-

This is to certify that JOHN HENRY HACKER, who is about to proceed to Canada, has been employed in the Wagon Department here as a Labourer since the 30th. March 1903.— He is leaving the service voluntarily today.

I have pleasure in stating that Hacker is an industrious workman of good ability, is sober and honest, and bears a good general character.

G. Churchward

Chief Superintendent.

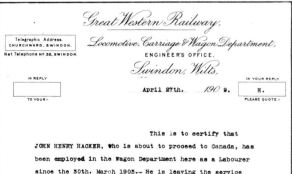

No. (3305)

GREAT WESTERN RAILWAY.

Swindon Works, 7ᵗʰ November 34

1178 F.B.Simpkins Your services will not be required after 5.30 p.m 7ᵗʰ December 1934

R.Hannington
Manager.

Attained 21 years

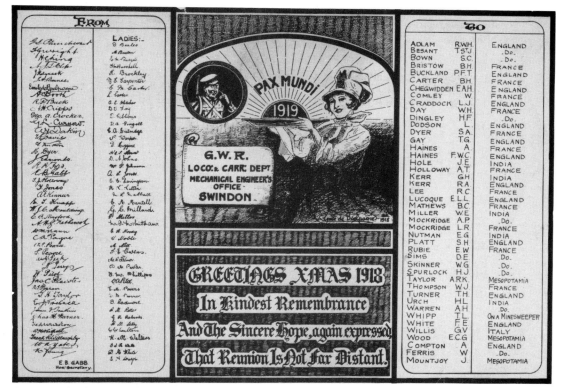

FROM				TO	

The card shows a list of names under "FROM" including "LADIES:" and is signed "E.B. GABB, Hon: Secretary." The central illustration reads "PAX MUNDI 1919", "G.W.R. LOCO: & CARR: DEPT. MECHANICAL ENGINEER'S OFFICE - SWINDON" and below "GREETINGS XMAS 1918 / In Kindest Remembrance / And The Sincere Hope, again expressed, / That Reunion Is Not Far Distant."

The "TO" list:

Name	Initials	Location
ADLAM	R.W.H.	ENGLAND
BESANT	T.S?J.	.Do.
BOWN	S.C.	.Do.
BRISTOW	B.H.	FRANCE
BUCKLAND	P.F.T.	ENGLAND
CARTER	B.H.	FRANCE
CHEGWIDDEN	E.A.H.	ENGLAND
COMLEY	W.	FRANCE
CRADDOCK	L.J.	ENGLAND
DAY	W.H.	FRANCE
DINGLEY	H.F.	.Do.
DODSON	L.	ENGLAND
DYER	S.A.	FRANCE
GAY	T.G.	ENGLAND
HAINES	A.	FRANCE
HAINES	F.W.C.	ENGLAND
HOLE	J.E.	INDIA
HOLLOWAY	A.T.	FRANCE
KERR	G.H.	INDIA
KERR	R.A.	ENGLAND
LEE	R.C.	FRANCE
LUCOQUE	E.L.L.	ENGLAND
MATHEWS	B.C.	FRANCE
MILLER	W.E.	INDIA
MOCKRIDGE	A.P.	.Do.
MOCKRIDGE	L.R.	FRANCE
NUTMAN	E.G.	INDIA
PLATT	S.H.	ENGLAND
RUBIE	E.W.	FRANCE
SIMS		.Do.
SKINNER	W.G.	.Do.
SPURLOCK	H.J.	.Do.
TAYLOR	A.R.K.	MESOPOTAMIA
THOMPSON	W.J.	FRANCE
TURNER	T.H.	ENGLAND
URCH	H.L.	INDIA
WARREN	A.H.	.Do.
WHIPP	T.L.	ON A MINESWEEPER
WHITE	F.E.	ENGLAND
WILLIS	G.V.	ITALY
WOOD	E.C.G.	MESOPOTAMIA
COMPTON	A.	ENGLAND
FERRIS	W.	.Do.
MOUNTJOY	J.	MESOPOTAMIA

An unusual Christmas greeting (above) from staff of the Chief Mechanical Engineer's office to their colleagues on military service, 1918. Some familiar Swindon names appear on both sides of the card

Christmas postcard from the staff of the general stores, 1950

39

Great Western Railway.

NOTICE !

SALE OF COAL TO COMPANY'S SERVANTS SWINDON.

From May 1st, 1932, the Haulage of Coal for Company's Servants in Swindon and Neighbourhood will be undertaken by the Company's Road Transport Department.

On and from the same date, an inclusive Flat Rate will be charged for Coal.

DELIVERY CHARGES WILL BE ABOLISHED
WITHIN THE BOROUGH
AND SHOULD NOT BE PAID.

The following Reduced Rates for delivery beyond the Borough Boundaries will come into effect at the same time.

			Per Cwt.
Badbury	-	-	2d.
Blunsdon	-	-	2d.
Chiseldon	-	-	2d.
Coate	-	-	½d.
Elcombe	-	-	2½d.
Hannington	-	-	3¼d.
Haydon Wick	-	-	1d.
Hodson	-	-	2d.
Hyde	-	-	1½d.
Kingsdown	-	-	1d.
Liddington	-	-	2d.
Lydiard Millicent	-	-	2½d.
Nine Elms	-	-	1¼d.
Shaw	-	-	1½d.
South Marston	-	-	1½d.
Stanton	-	-	3¼d.
Stanton Fitzwarren	-	-	3¼d.
Stratton	-	-	1d.
Wanborough	-	-	2d.
Washpool	-	-	1½d.
Wroughton—Borough Boundary to Perry's Lane	-		½d.
Wroughton—Perry's Lane and beyond			1d.

LOST TICKETS.

All Lost Tickets must be reported within One Month of their date.

April, 1932.   **BY ORDER.**

PRINTED BY THE SWINDON PRESS LTD., NEWSPAPER HOUSE, SWINDON.

GREAT WESTERN RAILWAY.

CONVEYANCE OF FIREWOOD

FOR WORKMEN USING THE PURTON WORKMEN'S TRAIN.

Commencing on Thursday next, the 17th instant, Workmen requiring Firewood or Old Timber conveyed to PURTON must load the Wood during the dinner hour into a Truck which will be placed in the Water Siding at the Junction Station.

This truck will be worked to Purton during the afternoon and placed in the Sidings there to enable the Wood to be unloaded.

In future no Wood will be conveyed by the Workmen's Train.

BY ORDER

SWINDON.
Mon., 14th December, 1931.

Employment at Swindon Works was not without its perks, however minor, cheap coal and firewood being generally available (left) from coal wharfs in Station Road and Rodbourne Road, and the wood wharf in Whitehouse Road

Below: GWR and BR(W) telephone code cards for the internal circuits to Bristol and Uffington

Great Western Railway. (3690)

Telephone Circuit between Bristol and No. 1 Bus Circuit Swindon

STATIONS.	CODE-CALLS. (RINGS)
Bristol Exchange	3 - 1
Bath T.O.	5 - 3
" Inspectors	6 - 1
Bathampton S.M.O.	4 - 2
Farleigh Down Checkers	2 - 1
Box S.M.O.	2 - 3
Corsham S.M.O.	5 - 4
Thingley Jcn. Inspectors	4 - 1
Chippenham West Box	2 - 2
" " B.O.	6 - 4
" " T.C.	1 - 3
" " Shunters	1 - 1
" " P.W. Inspector	1 - 4
" " Goods Office	2 - 4
" " East Box	6 - 2
Swindon West Box	8 - 1
" " T.O.	5 - 1
" " Exchange	7 - 1
Chippenham Loco	4 - 4
Dauntsey Office	4 - 3
Christian Malford	4 - 5

BRITISH RAILWAYS (Western Region) (3690)

Telephone Circuit between Challow Box and Swindon West Box.

STATIONS	CODE-CALLS (RINGS)
~~Challow Box~~	~~1-1~~
Uffington Box	1-2
Knighton Xing Box	2-1
Ashbury Xing Box	2-2
Shrivenham Box	~~~~ 2-3
Marston ~~West~~ East	~~~~ 6-3
Highworth Jcn. Box	5-1
Swindon Goods Yard Box	6-1
Swindon Goods Yard Inspr.	5-2
Swindon East Box	6-2
Swindon Telegraph Office	~~~~ 1-1
Swindon West Box	8-1
Swindon Works Exchange	7-1
Marston West	1-4

Swindon Strike Bulletin

THE LATEST AND TRUE FACTS OF THE STRIKE SITUATION

No. 2. WEDNESDAY, OCTOBER 1st, 1919. ONE PENNY.

Dear Comrades,

At the time of writing we find it impossible to make any definite arrangements as regards to ensuring the 'Daily Herald' being brought to Swindon for to-day's issue. We feel certain that we shall succeed in obtaining a supply for Thursday.

REPORTS FROM STRIKE CENTRES.

Wootton Bassett. Solidarity and good spirits reign here.
Newport. Absolutely solid.
Newton Abbot. Out to a man.
Chippenham. Splendid solidarity, 98% all grades out.
Westbury. Magnificent solidarity.
Cirencester. Astounding success, absolutely solid.
Gloucester. 1310 on strike out of 1325.
Lydney. Only three working.

Telegram received from **Brighton** :—

Every shop worker out here, traffic also, position splendid. Wires from other centres state same position.

RAYNER
Sec. Shop Workers' National Committee.

The following reports were received by 'phone at midnight.—

Welshpool. Confidence not shaken.
Exeter. All standing firm.
Derby. Position excellent. District solid including shopmen.
Plymouth. Top hole. All out.

Our old friend George Brown wiring from **Bristol** states "position splendid from Bristol to Weymouth," and the Bristol Secretary wires, "all grades responded magnificently."

SWINDON.

The Strike Committee are satisfied with the magnificent response. If members loyal success is assured, above reports give greatest confidence. **We are bound to win.**

SWINDON'S WATER SUPPLY.

The Strike Committee are surprised to learn of the shortage of water in the district served from the G.W.R. Pumping Station at Kemble. The N.U.R., men there have not been on strike and intimation was given to the G.W.R. Co., by resolution passed on Saturday last, that permission would be given to the N.U.R. members to maintain the water supply.

Instructions have to-day been issued to the N.U.R. members at the pumping station that they are to pump 100,000 gallons of water to Swindon and the necessary supply to Kemble.

Special Report from " Daily Herald " office

The constituent unions of the Triple Alliance will meet at eleven o'clock on Wednesday to discuss the support to be given to the Railwaymen.

The Government announce that a restricted service is being maintained by the help of volunteer labour, but it is evident that little improvement is taking place.

The Transport Workers have issued a splendid message to the effect that they can do no other than support the Railwaymen.

Armed troops are protecting both of the London Power Stations, and men with machine guns are encamped in Regent's Park. In spite of these flagrant displays of the Government's intentions the spirit of the men remains splendid and three of the largest meetings ever held in London have been addressed by the leaders to-day.

The Postal Workers, The Vehicle Workers, and the Printing Trades have decided not to black-leg or to touch black work.

TO-DAYS' TIT BIT.

Bradford, Yorks, wires :—
GO TO BED " JIMMY " FOR A WEEK.
ALL WELL HERE.

ANNOUNCEMENTS.

Football at Rodbourne Recreation Ground at 3.0 p.m., to-day.
A.S.L.E. & F. *v* J. Shop Moulders.
Women Workers Meeting, 2.30 p.m., to-day, Lecture Hall.
Picketts Duties for Thursday, Friday and Saturday will be Exhibited Wednesday and Thursday.
Ladies Pair Gold Spectacles. Will the Person who took the spectacles from the mantle shelf in the kitchen of Committee Rooms, Please Return Here.

A bright and striking afternoon's Football was well appreciated and enjoyed by thousands of our strikers yesterday afternoon. The Married *v* Single Match was of intense interest. The collisions, long runs and the rolling of Scotty in the struggle for the ball caused great amusement.

On behalf of the Committee,

G. PULLIN.

LOCAL CO-OPERATIVE NOTES.

Trade Unionists, as Co-operator's, own in Swindon and District :—

12 Grocery and Provision Shops.
2 Drapery Shops.
Boot and Shoe, Outfitting, Furnishing and Hardware Dept.
Boot and Shoe repairing Shop.
A Coal Wharf.
Large **Warehouses,** Motor Cars and Lorry's.

They are doing a trade of nearly £5,000 per week. They also have an up-to-date Bakery of the very latest pattern, Nationalisation is a form of co-operation. why not own the Railways Co-operatively and stop strikes ?

Pay 1/- entrance fee and join the twin movement of Trade Unionism.

CHARLES E. TAYLOR.

Printed by John Drew (Printers) Ltd , 51. Bridge Street, Swindon, and Published by Strike Committee, Co-op Hall, Harding Street.

Swindon Strike Bulletin

THE LATEST AND TRUE FACTS OF THE STRIKE SITUATION

No. 3. THURSDAY, OCTOBER 2ND, 1919. ONE PENNY.

HOLD FAST. RALLY TO RAILWAYMEN

DEAR COMRADES,

Every hour that passes by is forcing a tighter bond of Comradeship which will inevitably take possession of the means of Production. The functions of the Capitalist serves no purpose and we were again made aware of the fact, when we paid at the rate of only 10d. per quart for milk this morning : over 200% increase on pre-war prices. We are not surprised to hear the reported remarks made by Mr. Tyrrell, M.P., of the Chippenham Division, speaking to-day at Cricklade, when he advised the people to Boycott the Strikers and prevent them from obtaining rations, presumably Mr. Tyrrell is not aware that the prices do that. He was asking for trouble and deserved even more than being chased off the platform. He also stated to one of our strikers, if he would return to work he would secure for him a good job on the Railway for the remainder of his career.

Don't be intimidated Comrades, don't be led away NOW (or at election times) by such a man taking a line which is very dangerous to the whole community. Remember we are not out to accept sops, or be bought off neither divided by such despicable baits. We are struggling to rise the "Bottom Dog," and the fact that a large number of men on the Railway in the better position (such as they are) prepared to sacrifice their all. It shews this great spirit of Comradeship has taken good root and the seed has grown into the flower of truth, and the truth is that the conduct of a good Railwayman is first. To his fellow Worker.

The general situation is improving, so ran the official statement issued from Downing Street on Monday last. Yesterday one of the leading London Dailies referred to the **Growing Chaos.** The position has so far improved from our standpoint that the " Daily Mail " which since Friday last has used every endeavour to discredit our leaders, has discovered that a statement of the Government's offer is necessary. If the ray of truth which has caused the " Daily Mail " to call for the clearing up of the doubt be followed, it will, we are sure, lead the Editor to the conclusion that there is much justice in our demands. " What the railwaymen's future wages are to be should " we agree " be settled now and made crystal clear."

" We are threatened by the **mis-understanding** or misdirection of the strikers, and the recklessness of their leaders," says the " Daily Chronicle " which sees nothing but a catastrophe in the possibility of our strike meeting with success. The prominence given by this journal to the fact that duchesses, countesses and lords CAN work must not and be lost sight of in later days. Costly furs and expensive jewellery were in evidence at one black-leg depot, probably bought out of the profits made on the nation's food supply, no wonder, " keep smiling." We read " for five years they have been accustomed to crises," to such people a " crisis " is but an inconvenience, while we are faced with one each time we have to buy a pair of boots for the kiddies, a suit for ourselves, or the wife has to buy the week's rations.

" The side which is losing or fears that it may lose is tempted to an ever increasing use of force " says the ' Manchester Guardian.' We are indebted to the ' Guardian ' for this explanation of the use of the military, and it should strengthen our members in their determination to **win through without resort to violence.**

It is interesting to note how the press, quite unintentionally no doubt, occasionally reply to their own question. The " Star " on Monday stated that the railwaymen's wages would be all spent, nothing left for furs and jewellery, and four day's food. This should answer the question as to the need for higher wages.

SUPPORT FROM EX-SOLDIERS.

At their monthly meeting at the Town Hall on Tuesday evening the members of the Swindon Branch of the Comrades of the Great War passed a resolution to the effect that they will not assist in strike breaking in any form and that they will remain loyal to their respective trade unions.

REPORT.

All reports from strike centres indicate that the men are remaining loyal to their E.C's, and are determined to win. The women are in this fight, and an enthusiastic meeting of the Swindon Members was held yesterday. Mrs. Prosser presided, and it was decided to hold a further meeting in the Lecture Hall at 2.30 p.m., on Friday.

The excellent programme given in the Mechanics' Institute on Tuesday evening was rivalled by the A.S.L.E. & F. Concert at the Riflemans Hotel last night. The arrangements were well carried out by the Entertainments Committee, who have secured the use of the Wesley Institute, Faringdon Street, for recreation purposes from Thursday at 3.0 p.m., and each day following from 10 a.m., to 9 p.m.

The football match between the A.S.L.E.& F., and the Moulders resulted in a win for the Enginemen by 6 goals to 2. Selections of music by the N.U.R.— Band were appreciated.

To-day's fixture :—G.W.R. *v* M. & S.W.J.R. Princes Street Recreation Ground 3.0 p.m.

STOP PRESS NEWS.

The Executive Committee met the Premier.

No Settlement was arrived at when the meeting closed long after Midnight.

The Executive Committee meeting again at Unity House, early this morning, when a further Conference will be held with the Prime Minister.

On behalf of the Strike Committee,

G. PULLIN.

Printed by John Drew (Printers) Ltd , 51. Bridge Street, Swindon, and Published by Strike Committee, Co-op Hall, Harding Street.

Left: two issues of the Swindon Strike Bulletin, relating to the nine-day national strike by railwaymen in October 1919. The strike reflected a wide ranging dissatisfaction in the aftermath of the First World War. High unemployment, shortage of housing and changing work practices were all causes of discontent, while railwaymen were further angered by the threat to withdraw war bonuses

Less than two months after the General Strike of 1926, a valuable publicity coup was pulled off by Sir Felix Pole, General Manager of the GWR, with the running of a special excursion train to Swindon for the delegates of the International Railway Congress (right). The start-to-stop timings (below) imitated those of the crack 'Cheltenham Flyer' express, although the scheduled 75 minute journey time was doubtless beaten on the return to Paddington

PADDINGTON TO SWINDON.

Distance from Paddington.			Principal Stations.	Times	Speed per hour		Remarks.
Miles	Chains	Kilo-metres.		p.m.	Miles	Kilo-metres.	
—	—	—	PADDINGTON...Dep.	1.10	—	—	
9	6	14·60	Southall pass	1.21	49· 5	79·66	
18	36	29·69	Slough ... „	1.29½	66·18	106·47	
24	19		Maidenhead ... „	1.34	69·45	111·72	
35	78	57·89	Reading ... „	1.45	67·07	107·94	
43	20	69·60	*Water Troughs*	—	—		Locomotive may take up water whilst running.
53	10	85·49	Didcot ... „	2. 1	64·31	103·49	
56	42	90·97	Steventon ... „	2. 4½	58·29	93·94	
77	24	124·40	SWINDON ... Arr.	2.25	60· 8	97·85	Delegates may rejoin Train in Works Siding at any time during the afternoon for tea if desired.
77	24	124·40	Overall	Mins. 75	61·84	99·52	

No. of Vehicles on train ... 9
Overall length excluding engine ... 630 ft. (283 metres.)
Weight of train (empty) excluding engine... 321 tons 14 cwt.

SWINDON TO PADDINGTON.

Distance from Swindon.			Principal Stations.	Times	Speed per hour		Remarks.
Miles	Chains	Kilo-metres.	Swindon—Loco. Works Siding	p.m.	Miles	Kilo-metres.	
			dep.	5.10			
—	—	—	SWINDON ... Dep.	5.25	—	—	Speed not to exceed 15 miles (24·14 Kilo-metres) per hour between 63 miles 40 chains and 60 miles 77 chains be-tween Challow and Wantage Road.
20	62	33·43	Steventon ... pass	5.45½	60· 8	97·85	
24	14	38·91	Didcot ... „	5.49	58·29	93·94	
34		54·71	*Water Troughs*	—		103·49	Locomotive may take up water whilst running.
41	26	66·50	Reading ... „	6. 5	64·31	107·94	Speed not to exceed 15 miles (24·14 Kilo-metres) per hour between 26 miles 62 chains and 26 miles 18 chains be-tween Twyford and Maidenhead.
53	5	85·39	Maidenhead „	6.15½	67·07		
58	68	94·71	Slough „	6.20½	69·45	111·72	
68	18	109·80	Southall „	6.29	66·18	106·47	Speed not to exceed 30 miles per hour between West-bourne Park Station and Ranelagh Bridge.
77	24	124·40	PADDINGTON Arr.	6.40	49· 5	79·66	
77	24	124·40	Overall	Mins. 75	61·84	99·52	

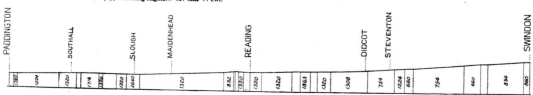

NEWBURN,
CHORLEYWOOD ROAD,
RICKMANSWORTH,
HERTS.

TEL: 2131

June 1st 1962

Dear Mr Scott,

Many thanks to you & the Swindon Staff for the Birthday Greetings & Good Wishes which arrived for my Birthday anniversary.

I am afraid there are not many left who knew me when I left.

But an impression 40 years deep is not readily lost.

& kindest regards

Sincerely yours

W A Stanier

Letter from Sir William Stanier to J.S. Scott, Chief Works Manager at Swindon, 1962. It reads, 'Many thanks to you and the Swindon Staff for the Birthday Greetings and Good Wishes which arrived for my Birthday anniversary. I am afraid there are not many left who knew me when I left. But an impression 40 years deep is not readily lost.' This was Stanier's ninetieth birthday; he had left the GWR in 1931. His Rickmansworth address must surely have reflected his aspirations at Swindon which were never fulfilled: to become Chief Mechanical Engineer of the GWR and to reside at Newburn House

Great Western Railway.

On SUNDAY, Feb. 7th,

A HALF-DAY EXPRESS
EXCURSION will run to

LONDON

Leaving	At	Return Fares, Third Class.	
BRISTOL—	A.M.	From BRISTOL Stations	6/-
Bedminster	11 0		
Temple Meads	11 10		
Clifton Down	10 40		
Montpelier	10 45	From BATH	5/6
Stapleton Road	10 50		
Lawrence Hill	10 55		
BATH	11 30		
	P.M.	From SWINDON	5/-
SWINDON	12 15		
	P.M.		
Paddington arr.	1 52		

The RETURN TRAIN will leave PADDINGTON STATION at 9.20 p.m. the same day.

TAKE YOUR TICKET IN ADVANCE.

Excursion notice, 1926. The fare from Swindon was 5 s.

Everything first class at Swindon

Right: Edwardian comic postcard

G. W. R.
NOTICE.

SALE OF OLD TIMBER AND "REFUSE" TIMBER TO STAFF

In future the price of Wood Tickets will include the charge for delivery to consumers' premises.

Prices for Old Timber and "Refuse" Timber Tickets will be as follows :--

	PER CWT.
BOROUGH OF SWINDON AND ADJACENT DISTRICTS (OTHER THAN INDICATED BELOW)	2/=
CHISELDON LIDDINGTON ELCOMBE WROUGHTON WANBOROUGH PURTON AREA, including Lydiard Millicent, Lydiard Green and Hook WOOTTON BASSETT AREA, including Ballards Ash, Broadtown, Vastern and Black Dog HIGHWORTH AREA, including Hannington and Stanton Fitzwarren	2/3

A delivery programme will be arranged by the Stores Department but no guaranteed date of delivery can be given.

When delivery is effected, the purchaser should give his portion of the ticket to the Carter in exchange for the Haulier's portion in the same way as for Coal. It is suggested that Tickets should be left accessible to the Carter when the house is unoccupied, otherwise delivery may be delayed until the next ticket is dealt with.

The Hauliers engaged under contract are :--

Messrs. W. F. COLE and SONS,
11 Hunt Street, Swindon.
For deliveries within the Borough of Swindon.

Mr. F. L. BELCHER,
7 Northdown Avenue,
Kingsdown, Nr. Swindon.
For deliveries outside the Borough of Swindon.

The first issue of tickets will be dated 12th January, 1948, and will be limited to 1 cwt. of Refuse or 1 cwt of Old Timber.

H. R. WEBB,
Stores Superintendent's Office,
Swindon.

F. W. HAWKSWORTH,
Chief Mechanical Engineer's Office,
Swindon.

20th December, 1947.

JOHN DREW (PRINTERS) LTD., SWINDON

G.W.R. STAFF ASSOCIATION
(SWINDON DIVISION)
President - - F. W. HAWKSWORTH, Esq.

THEATRICAL SECTION

A

MEETING

WILL BE HELD ON

Wednesday, 5th June, 1946
AT 7-30 P.M., IN THE LARGE HALL AT

THE INSTITUTE, BRIDGE STREET
TO CONSIDER THE FORMATION OF AN

OPERATIC SECTION

ALL MEMBERS INTERESTED
ARE CORDIALLY INVITED TO ATTEND

NON-ASSOCIATION MEMBERS may attend provided their Names and Addresses are submitted to the General Secretary at least 48 hours beforehand.

Your active Support is earnestly requested in this effort of the Swindon Division to provide another Activity for its Members.

Are **YOU** a Member? If not, fill in the 1d. per week Paybills Deduction Form for Membership and Share in the Activities. Wives of Members may Join the Association for the Small Fee of 1/- per Year. See Your Shop Representative for Full Particulars.

H. A. MILES, General Secretary

A selection of posters from the post-war years (right, and preceding pages.). Note that the design of these letterpress notices varied little, whether issued by the GWR management, the Staff Association or BR Western Region. Since the early days of the GWR in Swindon, it had been accepted practice to sub-contract the printing of such items to local jobbing printers, and the names of Twitcher & Co., Drew, the Borough Press and Victoria Press regularly appear at the foot of notices issued by or on behalf of the GWR Works. Many retained a distinctly Victorian typographical quality, even in the British Railways era, and it is surprising that the Works management did not ever see fit to invest in their own printing presses for such purposes

BRITISH RAILWAYS · WESTERN REGION
Chief Mechanical Engineer's
Staff and Correspondence Offices

*

THIRTY-SEVENTH
Annual Dinner

Friday, January 30th, 1948
7 p.m. for 7.15 p.m.

OXFORD HOTEL · SWINDON

*

In the Chair : Mr. H. W. Gardner

A. W. Done, Hon. Sec.

Programme of Toasts & Music

Part I.

1. Toast: "The King, Queen, Queen Mary, and other Members of the Royal Family"
   The Chairman
2. Piano Medley - At the Piano - A. E. S. Fluck
3. Song - "King Charles" - *Maud Valerie White*
   Alfred Salter
4. Gloucestershire Humour
   Chick Fowler
5. Song - "Romance" - *Romberg*
   Beryl Done
6. Toast: "The British Railways, Western Region"
   Proposer: Mr. T. H. Turner
   To respond: Mr. F. W. Hawksworth
7. Some Magic
   Horace King and Betty
8. Duet - "Fold your Wings" - *Ivor Novello*
   Beryl Done and Alfred Salter

INTERVAL OF 15 MINUTES

Part II.

1. Sing-Song - At the Piano - A. E. S. Fluck
2. Song - "The Dancing Lesson" - *Teschemacher*
   Beryl Done
3. Dialect Humour
   Chick Fowler
4. Duet "I'll Walk beside You" *Allan Murray*
   Beryl Done and Alfred Salter
5. Toast: "Former Colleagues"
   Proposer: Mr. B. H. Carter
   To respond: Mr. H. Perry, Mr. W. M. Nunn
   and others
6. More Magic
   Horace King and Betty
7. "Rose Marie" - *Rudolf Friml*
   Alfred Salter

Accompanist - A. E. S. Fluck

Programme for the CME's Annual Dinner, 1948. Unusually the Oxford Hotel had been chosen in preference to the normal venue, the Goddard Arms. On this date, the newly-formed British Railways was just one month old, and the second toast – replacing the time-honoured 'The GWR Company' – must have stuck in the throat of many a diner

Inside and Outside the Works

A selection of views from within the GWR Works and around the railway village.

This well-known photograph, looking west from Swindon station, depicts the GWR Works in mixed gauge days and shows the original carriage shops (left), the erecting shop and general offices (centre), and the original Medical Fund swimming baths adjacent to the North Wilts Canal (right)

An aerial view of the carriage and wagon shops to the north of the station in 1924, with sidings full of rolling stock, looking north-east to Ferndale Road and St Mary's Grove

Aerial photographs of the railway workshops, 1920. Above: the huge 'A' erecting shop, looking north-east, with the Weighbridge House in front and the terraces of Even Swindon beyond. The sidings between the weighbridge and the wheel shop (left) were a favourite location for official locomotive photographs. Newburn House, home of the chief mechanical engineers of the GWR, stands in the foreground. The view below, looking north-west from above Swindon junction, shows the main office buildings and nucleus of the original locomotive works, with the carriage shops to the left and the erecting shop in the distance

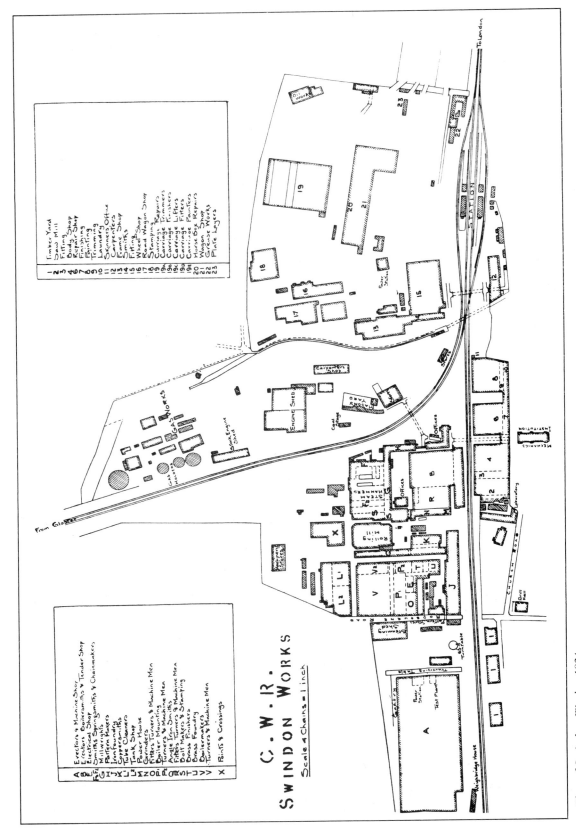

Plan of Swindon Works, 1924

Looking east towards Swindon junction, this official British Railways view dates from the early 1950s, and is taken from the top of the telephone exchange building, with the main offices to the left and carriage shops to the right

The changing panorama from the pattern shop roof, looking over the Works turntable towards 'A' shop in 1945 (top left), 1977 (bottom left), 1985 (above) and 1989 (below)

Locomotives under repair in 'A' shop in this 1912 postcard view include 'Saint' class No. 2924 *Saint Helena*, 'Flower' class No. 4109 *Lobelia*, 2–6–2 tank engine No. 4521 and 2–8–0 goods engine No. 2811. Commercial photographers were normally only permitted into the Works on Sundays, hence the lack of activity in this picture

The steam hammer shop, 1912: another study from the lens of William Hooper

'Hall' class No. 5975 *Winslow Hall* in 'A' shop, 1947

A locomotive boiler photographed after repair outside the boiler mounting shop, 1938, *en route* to nearby 'A' shop

The eight prominent chimneys of the central boiler station, with the twin domes of the Works hooter to the left

Inside Hooter House, 1977: ex-GWR clock No. 1851 (since privately preserved) still keeps 'railway time'

The twin brass domes of the Works hooter are still *in situ* on top of Hooter House, although they have remained silent since the closure of the Works in 1985

The GWR gasworks was originally opened within the original Locomotive Works in 1842; it was rebuilt in 1874 to the east of the Gloucester line, and subsequently extended in 1891 and during the 1920s due to increasing demand on capacity. These two official views date from around 1910 and show the southern end of the extended retort building. The lower photograph also includes the smaller oil gasworks building, with the construction of the new purifying house proceeding in the background. The gasworks finally closed in 1959

The gasworks can be seen in the background of this 1958 photograph, looking north-east from Swindon running sheds. To the right, the new points and crossings ('X') shop is under construction: destined to have a ridiculously short working life of only four years, 'X' shop was to be the last addition to Swindon Works

On display in the Works in 1961 are some of the skilfully-executed products from the pattern shop and foundry, including train headboards, 'Warship' class diesel engine name-plates and locomotive components

A feast of GWR name-plates still adorned the corridors of the main Works offices until closure in 1985. Plates from *The Great Bear*, *President*, *Alliance*, *City of Bath*, *Sultan* and *Bulldog* are now preserved by Swindon Railway Museum

The desolate scene in the wagon shops after closure, September 1967

Two 'posed' GWR publicity photographs, reproduced in photogravure for use in an official brochure, to demonstrate the lifting capacity of the 100-ton overhead crane in 'A' shop (above) and 36-ton breakdown cranes (below). The engine in the lower photograph is Churchward's experimental 4–6–2 No. 111 *The Great Bear*

The footpath and cycle track on the site of the North Wilts Canal, 1937, with the road vehicle shops to the left, looking south towards Sheppard Street

The imposing outline of Newburn House, built in 1873 for the use of Joseph Armstrong, Locomotive Superintendent of the GWR, and also the residence of his successors, William Dean and George J. Churchward. After his retirement in 1921, Churchward stayed at Newburn until his untimely death in 1933. C.B. Collett, Chief Mechanical Engineer after Churchward, declined to move into Newburn House, preferring instead the more manageable house in Church Place, shown below in 1927

Adjacent to Collett's residence were the formal gardens and cricket-ground of the GWR Park, shown here looking towards St Mark's Church. Note the ornamental fountain, which is of the same design as that in front of the Medical Fund Hospital (p. 22)

London Street in the railway village, looking west towards the Mechanics' Institute, with the carriage shops to the right

A motor bus outing for the employees of 'R' shop, June 1912, awaiting departure from the rear of the Mechanics' Institute. Unusually, the transport is provided by buses from Bath Electric Tramways' fleet

Members of the Associated Society of Locomotive Engineers, Firemen and Cleaners proudly display their banner in the leafy surrounds of Beckhampton Street Recreation Ground, c. 1920

The Royal Visit

The first visit of royalty to Swindon took place on 28 April 1924 when King George V and Queen Mary spent an afternoon in the town, with a guided tour of the railway works providing the main attraction. Her Majesty, in particular, was said to have shown 'keen interest' in the Works.

Opposite: two press photographs showing the king and queen's departure from the Works on the footplate of 'Castle' class engine No. 4082 *Windsor Castle*, with the king 'at the controls' and senior officers of the GWR in attendance. Note the queen's precaution against oily hands

Route and timetable of the royal visit, as published in a souvenir brochure (right). An expression of their majesties' thanks (below) to Viscount Churchill, Chairman of the GWR

WINDSOR CASTLE.

28th April, 1924.

Dear Churchill,

The King and Queen wish me to thank you and your Staff for to-day's excellent arrangements at Swindon.

It was gratifying to Their Majesties to have this opportunity of becoming acquainted with this vast industrial centre and of seeing the various departments of the well-known Works of your Company.

The King and Queen have carried away the happiest recollections of their first visit to Swindon, and they much appreciated the loyal reception extended to them while proceeding on the engine "Windsor Castle" from Weighbridge to the Station, by the thousands of men and women upon whose skill and efficiency the prosperity and development of this important Railway Headquarters so largely depends.

Yours sincerely,

Clive Wigram

The Viscount Churchill, G.C.V.O.,

Route and Time Table

2.10 P.M.	*Arrive at* SWINDON STATION
2.15 P.M.	*Drive from* SWINDON STATION *by way of*
	FLEET STREET
	BRIDGE STREET
	REGENT STREET
	REGENT CIRCUS (Post Office side)
2.20 P.M.	CENOTAPH
	TOWN HALL
	VICTORIA ROAD
	WOOD STREET
	HIGH STREET
	NEWPORT STREET
	DEVIZES ROAD
	BATH ROAD
	to VICTORIA HOSPITAL
2.45 P.M.	*Inspection of* VICTORIA HOSPITAL
3.0 P.M.	*Leave* VICTORIA HOSPITAL *for* SWINDON WORKS *by way of* BATH ROAD
	VICTORIA ROAD
	REGENT STREET
	BRIDGE STREET
	FARRINGDON STREET
3.10 P.M.	G.W.R. MEDICAL FUND SURGERY AND BATHS
	ACCIDENT HOSPITAL
	MECHANICS' INSTITUTION
3.15 P.M.	SWINDON WORKS
	Enter Works by SHEPPARD STREET ENTRANCE
	INSPECT LAUNDRY
	POLISHING AND FINISHING SHOPS
	CARRIAGE BODY-MAKING
	SAW MILL
	IRON FOUNDRY
	ENGINE BEING TURNED ON BALANCED TURNTABLE BY ONE MAN
	TYPES OF ENGINES IN YARD
	ENGINE TESTING PLANT
	GENERAL MACHINE SHOP
	ENGINE ERECTING SHOP
	LIFTING COMPLETE ENGINE BY OVERHEAD CRANE
	WHEEL SHOP
	WHEEL BALANCING
	WEIGHBRIDGE AND ENGINE BEING WEIGHED
4.25 P.M.	*Entrain* ROYAL SALOON (*outside Weighbridge House*) *to be drawn by the* "WINDSOR CASTLE."
4.30 P.M.	*Leave* SWINDON STATION

Railwaymen in Camera

The GWR created an industrial community in the heart of the Wiltshire countryside which contained much energy and collective enthusiasm for social welfare and self-improvement. Much of this spirit is revealed in the many group photographs of Swindon railwaymen during both the GWR and BR eras.

Carriage and wagon ambulance class, 1898

St John's Ambulance Association, Swindon GWR team, 1913/14

St John's Ambulance Association: squads taking part in a display at the Victoria Hospital, Swindon, June 1899

69

Second World War ARP factory wardens in the GWR carriage works, pictured in both uniform and civilian dress, *c.* 1940

A fine study of chief officers and drawing office staff, *c.* 1925. Frederick Hawksworth, at that time Chief Draughtsman and later to become Chief Mechanical Engineer, is eighth from right in the second row

June 1950: K.J. Cook, Mechanical and Electrical Engineer (seated, centre), and H. Randle, Carriage and Wagon Engineer (seated, third from left), with senior Works officers, photographed outside the main offices at Swindon

The GWR always encouraged cultural activities, particularly music. A male voice choir was formed in 1919 and took part in many festivals and eisteddfods throughout the country. Above: award-winning GWR mixed choirs. Below: a less formal group, the Swindon GWR Harmonica Knights, *c.* 1936

Swindon's Brunel Singers who took part in the BR Staff Association Festival at Reading, March 1959

A farewell gathering and presentation to Mr Fred Forest of carriage and wagon No. 12 shop upon his retirement, 1963

Personal staff of the Chief Mechanical Engineer at their annual dinner, 6 January 1950. The venue is the main ballroom of the Goddard Arms Hotel. On the top table are the retiring CME, Frederick Hawksworth (seventh from left) and to his immediate left the new Mechanical and Electrical Engineer, K.J. Cook. The Master of Ceremonies, T.H. Turner, is to Mr Cook's left. Standing to the far right and first from right are two future mayors of Swindon: Harold Gardner (mayor in 1953/54) and A.W.J. Dymond (mayor in 1965/66 and also featured in photographs on pp. 129 and 131 of this book). To Mr Dymond's immediate right is Hugh Randle, Carriage and Wagon Engineer. This was the thirty-ninth and final CME's Dinner; in following years joint functions were held in conjunction with the Carriage and Wagon Engineer's office staff

Swindon's Pride

A selection from the photographic archives of Great Western steam.

This Gooch-designed engine was one of the first narrow gauge passenger locomotives to run on the GWR. Despite being of distinctive Great Western design, No. 69 *Avon* was, in fact, built by Beyer-Peacock with a 2–2–2 wheel arrangement, in 1855. Rebuilt in 1886, it was finally withdrawn in 1907

Dean 'Single' 4–2–0 No. 3046 *Lord of the Isles*, built at Swindon in 1895 for the purpose of hauling the heavy West Country expresses. Notice the family resemblence between this engine and No. 69 (above), despite the forty years difference in age. *Lord of the Isles* perpetuated the name of the former broad gauge locomotive which had been withdrawn in 1884 and preserved by the GWR at Swindon until 1906, when it was suddenly scrapped, apparently at the whim of G.J. Churchward

Variations on a theme: tank engines designed by Dean and Collett. Above: 'Buffalo' class saddle-tank No. 1601, built at Swindon in 1879 and withdrawn, after conversion to a pannier-tank, in 1931. Below: auto-fitted 0–4–2T No. 4800, the first of its class, built at Swindon in 1932 and seen here at the west end of the erecting shop

Awaiting attention at Swindon Works in BR days are (above) 'Saint' class No. 2937 *Clevedon Court*, and (below) 'Star' class No. 4061 *Glastonbury Abbey*

Here 0–6–0 goods engines spanning nearly seventy years. This page: Armstrong-designed No. 788 of 1873 vintage, photographed in front of the pattern shop in 1902. Opposite page: Collett's more austere approach is evident on '2251' class No. 2211, photographed as new in 1940 with blanked-out cab windows and unlined livery

Resplendent 'Star' No. 4015 *Knight of St John* stands by the Works turntable after overhaul during the 1930s

Two maids-of-all-work, both photographed at the same location, the sidings to the west end of the erecting shop. Churchward 2–8–2T No. 7200 of 1934 stands resplendent in the sun (above), while 'Hall' class No. 4998 *Eyton Hall* suffers from the combined effects of a light snowfall and retouched white background (below)

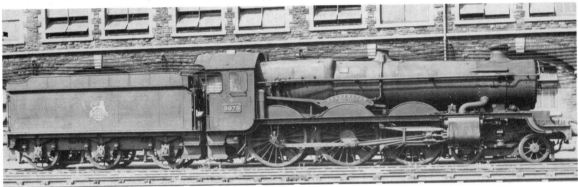

A trio of 'Castles' at Swindon in later years (top to bottom): No. 5057 *Earl Waldegrave* on display in 'A' shop as part of the exhibition organized to coincide with the naming ceremony of *Evening Star* in 1961 (this engine was scrapped a mere three years later); No. 5075 *Wellington* outside the foundry, awaiting entry into the Works; and No. 7037 *Swindon*, named at the Works by Princess Elizabeth in 1950

No. 7037 *Swindon* was the last in the line of 171 'Castle' class locomotives to be built at Swindon by the GWR and British Railways over a period of twenty-seven years. Close-up photographs of the splasher coat-of-arms (right) and the name-plate (below) reveal the presence of 'Achilles' class No. 3029 *White Horse* (wrongly numbered 2014) on the Borough crest. The incorporation of the crossed hammers and winged wheel into the design of the coat-of-arms is symbolic of the importance of the GWR Works to the town's economy

'Castle' No. 7037 proved to be a consistently poor steamer and was based at Swindon shed (code 82C) until withdrawal in 1953 (above). A *Swindon* of a previous era was 'Bulldog' class No. 3384 (originally No. 3446), built in 1903 and withdrawn in 1936 (below)

On Swindon shed during the 1950s is '5700' class pannier-tank No. 8723 (left)

Driver Albert Watts of Swindon shed with fireman, on the footplate of 0–6–0 mixed traffic engine No. 3203

Steam for scrap: among the many hundreds of GWR engines to end their days in the ignominious surroundings of the Works concentration yard were 'Bulldog' class No. 3380 *River Yealm* (left) and 'Dean Goods' No. 2541 (right)

The might and majesty of Great Western locomotive design at its peak: 'King' class No. 6000 *King George V* standing outside its birthplace in the late 1920s

Fourteen years after nationalization and No. 6003 *King George IV*, fresh from overhaul, is still turned out in GWR lined Brunswick green livery, with only the BR tender transfer and smokebox plates to spoil the overall Great Western effect

The end of an age: No. 92220 *Evening Star*, the last steam locomotive to be built for British Railways, pictured after the naming ceremony at Swindon on 18 March 1960

Act of preservation: 'Dean Goods' locomotive No. 2516 is seen on 1 April 1962 in Faringdon Road, *en route* from the Transfer Yard to GWR Museum

Gingerly reversing No. 2516 into its new resting-place at Swindon. Note the old Medical Fund Hospital buildings in the background, with the 1927 'temporary' extension in front, on the site of the garden pictured on p. 22.

The tender of No. 4003 *Lode Star*, also destined for the Museum, turns past Swindon station into Wellington Street, March 1962

Although steam remained supreme throughout the history of the GWR, the railway was not averse to experimenting with alternative forms of motive power.

This 70 bhp diesel-electric shunter was purchased in 1933 from John Fowler & Co. of Leeds. Identified as 'GWR No. 1' and painted in full lined-out livery, this engine was used for general shunting duties at Swindon Works

Streamlined diesel railcar No. 4 pictured at Swindon in 1960 after restoration. Built by AEC with Park Royal bodywork, No. 4 entered service in 1934 and was withdrawn in 1958. A later version of railcar was built by the GWR at Swindon from 1941. This photograph also shows examples of Swindon products from the BR era: 'Warship' class diesel-hydraulic locomotive, diesel multiple unit and Mark I coach

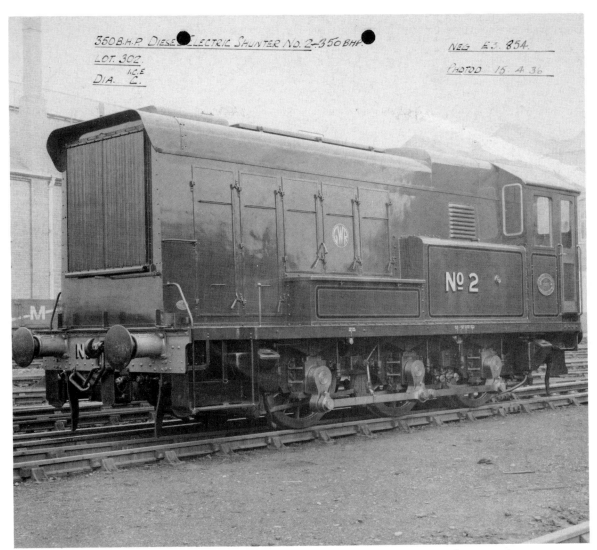

350 B.H.P. DIESEL ELECTRIC SHUNTER No. 2 – 350 BHP.

LOT. 302.

DIA. C.

NEG E.J. 854.

PHOTOD 15. 4. 36

GWR diesel–electric shunter No. 2, supplied by Hawthorn Leslie & Co. in 1935 for use at Acton Yard, seen here in a photograph from the Swindon files dated April 1936. This design was the forerunner of the standard BR class '08' shunter still in use today

In 1946 the GWR began looking seriously at alternatives to steam traction and placed orders for two gas-turbine locomotives. These were not supplied until the early 1950s, by which time the impetus of the original GWR idea had been halted by nationalization, and the possibilities of the gas-turbine concept were never explored to the full by British Railways. Pictured at Swindon Works are No. 18000 (above), supplied by Brown–Boveri of Switzerland and seen here consigned to a siding in 1955; and No. 18100 (below), supplied by Metro-Vickers and photographed outside 'A' shop in 1952

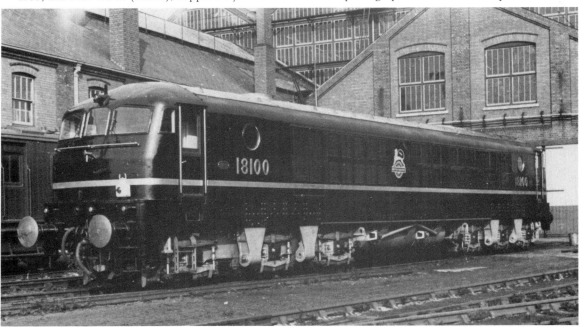

Passing Through

Paddington to Fishguard express passing through Swindon junction, September 1906, hauled by the experimental Churchward 4–6–0, No. 98. This engine, hailed as a milestone in locomotive design, is generally regarded as the first true Churchward standard locomotive. Note the varied collection of rolling stock, including clerestory and 'concertina' coaches

From the drawing office files is this 1946 photograph of 'Castle' class No. 5056 *Earl of Powis* heading a royal train out of Swindon towards Gloucester. This is an unusual photographic location, accessible only to railway officials: the North Yard of the Works, looking south towards the coaling stage and the main offices, with the spire of Christ Church just visible in the far distance

Another official photograph from 1946, with 'King' class No. 6003 *King George IV* passing the 'A' erecting shop with a down express. '2800' class No. 3855 is to the left

'Bulldog' class No. 3450 *Peacock* heads an up stopping train between Swindon and Didcot, *c.* 1912

Passing through Stratton Park Halt (above), 'Castle' class No. 7030 *Cranbrook Castle* heads the 11.45 a.m. Cheltenham to Paddington express on 4 March 1958

'King' class No. 6027 *King Richard I* pauses at Swindon on a Down express, *c.* 1950 (left). On the Up through road at Swindon junction, filthy 'Saint' class No. 2906 *Lady of Lynn* heads a freight train in April 1952 (below), shortly before its withdrawal from service

GWR workhorses pass through Swindon junction on a cold January day in 1952: vintage 'Dean goods' No. 2462 (above) on an Up train, and 'Hall' class No. 5919 *Worsley Hall* (below) viewed from platform 4 on a Down mixed goods service

High Days and Holidays

GWR Stores Department Staff Outing, June 1909, pictured aboard charabancs at Moretonhampstead. The day tour included a special train to Newton Abbot, a tour of Dartmoor and lunch at an hotel *en route*

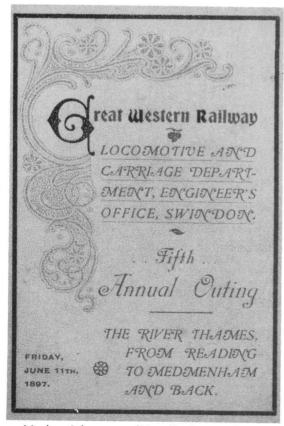

Much as July was traditionally the month of 'Trip', June was the month when the Works' annual outings took place. Here are two elegant Victorian outing programmes produced for the Engineer's Office

GREAT WESTERN RAILWAY . . . .

Locomotive & Carriage Department
Engineer's Office
Swindon

. Tenth .

Annual Outing

Saturday, 7th June, 1902

. To .

Shakespeare's
. . Country

". . . . Take him for all in all
We shall not look upon his like again."—
Hamlet.

- TIME TABLE -

Swindon G.W.R. (Saloon)   dep. 6·40 a.m.
Didcot   ..   ..   arr. 7·50 ,,
   ,, ...   dep. 8·13 ,,
Warwick   ..   ..   arr. 9·54 ,,
St. Mary's Church.
Warwick Castle.

"Much happier to live in a small house and have Warwick
Castle to be astonished at, than live in Warwick Castle and have
nothing to be astonished at."—*Ruskin.*

Dinner at "Woolpack" Hotel 12·0 noon
Warwick (Char-a-Banc)   dep. 12·45 p.m.
Charlecote Park.
Shottery (Ann Hathaway's Cottage).
Stratford-on-Avon   ...   arr. 2·45 ,,

Stratford-on-Avon.
Holy Trinity Church.
The Memorial Theatre.
Shakespeare's Birthplace.

Boating on River Avon.
Stratford-on-Avon G.W.R. dep. 5·20 p.m.
Leamington   ,,   arr. 6·2   ,,
Tea at "Crown" Hotel   6·15 ,,
Jephson Gardens.
(Band of the Royal Marine Artillery).
Leamington G.W.R.   ...   dep. 8·23 ,,
Oxford   ,,   ...   arr. 9·15 ,,
   ,,   ,,   ...   dep. 9·40 ,,
Didcot   ,,   ...   arr. 10·3 ,,
   ,,   ,,   ...   dep. 10·40 ,,
Swindon   ,,   ...   arr. 11·15 ,,

The cover and inner pages of another stylish Engineer's Office programme, 1902

Dressed to the nines: staff of the loco manager's office are immaculately attired for their annual excursion, 20 June 1914, although the location of this fine portrait is not recorded. The outbreak of the First World War was less than two months away, and one wonders how many of this proud group fell for 'King and Country' in the ensuing hostilities

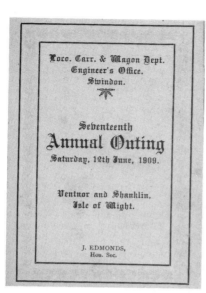

Loco. Carr. & Wagon Dept.
Engineer's Office,
Swindon.

Seventeenth
Annual Outing
Saturday, 12th June, 1909.

Ventnor and Shanklin,
Isle of Wight.

J. EDMONDS,
Hon. Sec.

❧ TIME TABLE. ❧

				A.M.
Swindon Town (saloons)	-	- dep.	6-25
Southampton Docks	-	- arr.	8-21
,,	(boat)	- dep.	9-20
Ryde	-	- arr.	10-20
,,	-	- dep.	10-26
Ventnor	-	- arr.	11-10
Lunch at Freemasons Hotel, High St.			12-30
Ventnor	-	- dep.	2-5
(or walk to Shanklin)		or	4-15
Shanklin	-	- arr.	2-15 or 4-27
Tea at Daish's Hotel, High St.			5-0
Shanklin	-	- dep.	6-52
Ryde	-	- arr.	7-22
,,	(boat)	- dep.	7-35
Southampton	-	- arr.	9-10
,,	(saloons)	- dep.	9-35
Swindon	-	- arr.	11-53

❧ ❧ MENUS. ❧ ❧

LUNCH.

Fish.

Roast Hindquarter of Lamb.

Mint Sauce.

Roast Beef.   Yorkshire Pudding.

Boiled Leg of Mutton.   Caper Sauce.

SWEETS.

Stewed Fruits.   Jellies.

Blanc Mange, etc.

Cheese.   Salad.

TEA.

Roast Beef.   Pressed Beef.

Brown and White Bread and Butter.

Cake.   Preserves.

Interestingly, this 1909 outing (above) made use of the rival M&SWJR's train service from Swindon Town to Portsmouth

Carriage and wagon staff aboard the *Empress of India* (left) at Windsor, during the riverborne leg of their outing, *c.* 1920

Selection of programme covers (below)

Great Western Railway
Locomotive & Carriage
Department
Engineer's Office,
Swindon

Eighth Annual . . . .
Outing

. . . June 16, 1900 . . .

Isle of Wight.

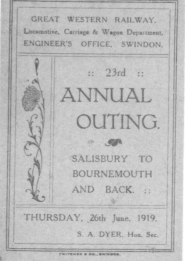

GREAT WESTERN RAILWAY.
Locomotive, Carriage & Wagon Department,
ENGINEER'S OFFICE, SWINDON.

:: 23rd ::
ANNUAL
OUTING.

SALISBURY TO
BOURNEMOUTH
AND BACK. ::

THURSDAY, 26th June, 1919.

S. A. DYER, Hon. Sec.

TWITCHER & CO., SWINDON.

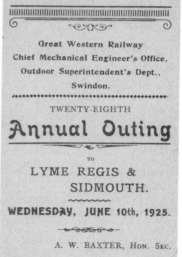

Great Western Railway
Chief Mechanical Engineer's Office,
Outdoor Superintendent's Dept.,
Swindon.

TWENTY-EIGHTH
Annual Outing
TO
LYME REGIS &
SIDMOUTH.

WEDNESDAY, JUNE 10th, 1925.

A. W. BAXTER, Hon. Sec.

Torquay provides the almost sub-tropical background for this 1932 photograph of the staff of the Locomotive Offices on their annual excursion

The Children's Fête, organized by the Committee of the Mechanics' Institution, was a major social event in the town's calendar. Commenced in 1868, it was held annually in the GWR Park until the outbreak of the Second World War, and normally took place on the second Saturday of August. From about 1880 onwards each child received on entry a packet containing a $\frac{1}{2}$lb slab of fruit cake and a free ticket for a roundabout ride.

As the fête grew in popularity, the cake-cutting became something of a problem. By 1890 the attendance had reached 20,000 and packing the pieces of cake was a time-consuming affair involving a large number of helpers. To alleviate the problem, the trimming shop foreman, Mr Harvie, designed an ingenious cake-cutting machine to speed up the laborious process. The machine made its debut in 1891, enabling over 2 tons of cake to be cut and wrapped within 4 hr.

The fête continued to expand: 38,000 attended the event in 1904, prompting the *Swindon Advertiser* to report in almost lyrical prose, 'The large enclosure simply bubbled over with a surging mass of bright, laughing humanity.' A popular feature of every fête was the photographer who would stand on a platform and take crowd shots which would later be displayed for sale in a side tent, fitting mementos of a great occasion for children and parents alike

Opposite page: a humorous postcard dating from 1906 showing crowds passing Park House on their way to the fête (top); and a William Hooper crowd shot, *c.* 1912 (bottom)

The cake-cutting ritual: volunteers at work in the Drill Hall before and after the introduction of Mr Harvie's labour-saving device

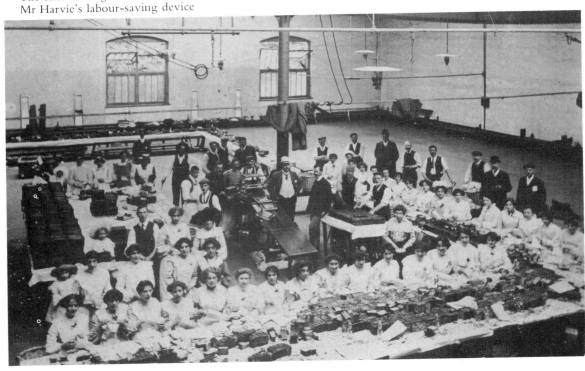

The GWR Works Fire Brigade

Two views of the Dennis fire-engine, with crew and fire-fighting paraphernalia, taken from Drawing Office blue-prints dated 24 November 1915. Engine No. 3 was delivered in 1912 to replace a stationary Merryweather engine, and remained in use until the 1940s. It is now preserved at the GWR Museum

Above: interior of the Bristol Street Fire Station prior to the First World War, showing both the Dennis and Merryweather engines. Note the call-board to the right of the picture, an ingenious device to alert off-duty firemen via links to bells which were installed in their houses in the nearby railway village. In the 1985 view, left, this board survives intact in precisely the same position

Mass Exodus

Postcard views of employees leaving the GWR Works were much favoured by local commercial photographers during the early part of this century. The cloth caps and grim faces of this vast army bring home the reality of working 'inside'. This view of the main Works entrance in London Street dates from *c.* 1908, and has been cleverly composed by the photographer, William Hooper, with urchins in the foreground and homeward-bound men literally stopped in their tracks

Above: another Hooper photograph, this time from a point adjacent to the carpenters shops and coal wharf in Station Road, looking eastwards. Below: Emlyn Square is shown in a late 1920s postcard view, with Taunton Street to the left and the Medical Fund hospital extension to the right

Tram No. 1 (above) edges its way through the throng heading towards Rodbourne Road bridges, *c.* 1906. A tinted postcard of 1908 (left) shows the dinner-time scene in Sheppard Street, with Compton's clothing factory to the right and the carriage shops in the distance

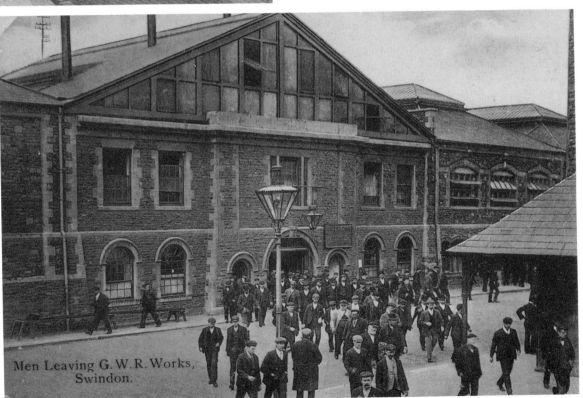

Men Leaving G.W.R. Works, Swindon.

The London Street entrance viewed from Emlyn Square, with a corner of the Mechanics' Institute to the right

A less photographed, though equally congested location: Whitehouse Road Carriage and Wagon Works entrance, pictured here during the 1940s outside the GWR laundry building. With the growth of the town, bicycles were a popular way of coping with the increased distances that many people faced to and from work, with the added advantage that they could also be used (as in this picture) for transporting home useful off-cuts of wood from the wood wharf in Whitehouse Road

The Mechanics' Institute

The GWR Mechanics' Institute was formed in 1844 as a social and educational group for the benefit of employees at Swindon Works and their families, the name of this organization later being applied to the building which was erected in 1855 on a parcel of land within the railway village. This building accommodated lecture and reading rooms, a dining hall, bathing facilities and an adjoining market.

Views of the Mechanics' Institute building, looking from Bristol Street towards Emlyn Square (above), *c.* 1920; and showing the 1893 extension on the former market site (below), *c.* 1910

An official GWR photograph of the main reading rooms in the 1893 extension (above). Note the wide range of newspapers and periodicals available to all members. Among the items on the rear wall is a portrait of Alfred Williams, local poet, essayist and author of *Life in a Railway Factory*, who was doubtless a member of the Institution while employed by the GWR from 1892 to 1914

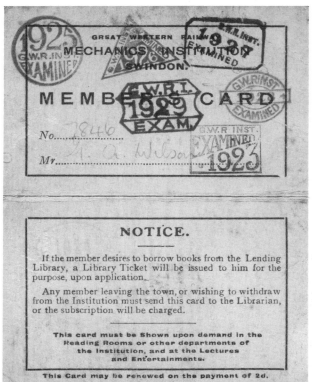

Left: Mechanics' Institute membership card, stamped for the years 1923–9

Interior views of the reference library (1931) (left) and the main lending library counter (below). While the fire extinguisher is of standard GWR design, the clock is by Deacon & Son, a local Swindon supplier

An architect's impression of the extended Institute building, 1892, as viewed from the corner of Reading Street. Brightwen Binyon was also the architect of Swindon's Town Hall

The Great Western Silver Band photographed outside the Mechanics' Institute in 1925. The officials in the front row are (left to right): C. Baker (conductor), W. Broome (vice-president), A.J.L. White (president) and T. Stanton (vice-president)

The Mayor of Swindon, Councillor S. Haskins, addresses the audience from the stage of the Mechanics' Institute's main hall, *c.* 1926. To his rear are the members of the GWR choir, and to his immediate right is William Stanier, at that time Works Assistant to the Chief Mechanical Engineer, C.B. Collett. Stanier was normally Collett's representative at functions such as this, due to the latter's well-known aversion to social activities

1990: this historic building now stands empty and neglected

Swindon Junction

The classic William Hooper postcard view of Swindon station forecourt, *c.* 1910. Among the hectic hustle and bustle are horse-drawn carts, traps, bicycles, Gregory Brothers' dairy float, Wm. McIlroy's delivery van and numerous pedestrians spilling around the corner into Station Road

Tinted Valentine's postcard view of Swindon station, looking west

Swindon has now become a great Depot for Terminal Trains — which have to be broken up & the traffic sorted for the various outward Trains — at all times it is not possible to carry out the instructions as to Marshalling & sending proper traffic by proper Trains — to remedy this a proper Fan shaped sorting & shunting Yd is required. this evil will become worse as the Traffic & Trains increase — the B.G. Cripple Sidings belonging to Traffic Dept. east of B Box — if narrowed & improved would suit admirably — Wm Bonner

A Blow pipe connection between the Bookg. office at Swindon — & the Tkt Collectors stationed on the Up & Down Platforms at the top of the Staircases — particularly the Up side — to prevent pass. being left behind after being booked. — some commn. of this kind is very much required —

An extract from a book entitled *Suggestions for Working Swindon Station*, which contains entries dating from between 1873 and 1886, is reproduced above. The book gives an insight into the problems involved in the day-to-day running of a busy junction station, bearing in mind the increasing importance of the locomotive factory and the continuing difficulties of mixed gauge working during that period.

The entries reveal problems such as the need for coke sheds at the east end of the station, inadequate pay for horse drivers (then employed for shunting purposes at Cocklebury yard) at 16 s. per week, the requirement for a stone crane at the transfer sidings and a narrow-gauge shunting engine in place of a broad gauge engine. Increases in staff numbers are evident during the late 1870s, with number-taking staff, a night yard foreman at the Transfer Yard, a station yard foreman and a lad clerk for the booking office all being recruited to deal with the increased workload.

Other improvements included the widening of Cocklebury Bridge (Whitehouse Road) in

1876, the installation of block telegraph between 'A' and 'B' signal boxes, the fixing of a compound crossing from the down branch line to the engine-house line near 'E' box, and the conversion of the Loco. siding between 'F' and 'E' cabins into a third road in preparation for the opening of the Severn Tunnel. Minor improvements at the station itself are also recorded, such as 'proper fittings' for the new guards and porters room, indicator boards 'to facilitate the movement of passengers obtaining access to Cloak Rooms, Lavatories, &c.', and extension of the verandahs covering the Up and Down platforms to prevent passengers being exposed to the weather 'which at times from the exposed position at Swindon is very severe'.

A selection of the entries is shown below, with the Station Superintendent's comments in italics:

More Carriage Siding Room is now required at the station and the removal of the Goods Shed to the Transfer Yd. is very necessary – more particularly now that the Loco. Dept. have taken two sidings from the station for Coaling purposes. Now that we have more through narrow-gauge Trains the removal of the Goods Shed is still further required – unable at present to transfer Vehicles from Down Main to Down Branch until after departure of Main Line Train. *Since Removed.*

Swindon has now become a great Depot for Terminal Trains which have to be broken up and the traffic sorted for the various outward Trains – at times it is not possible to carry out the instructions as to marshalling and sending proper traffic by proper Trains – to remedy this a proper Fan-shaped sorting and shunting Yd. is required. The evil will become worse as the Traffic and Trains increase: the broad gauge Cripple Sidings belonging to Traffic Dept. east of 'B' Box, if narrowed and improved, would suit admirably.

An additional Locking Gear Box is now required on the Gloster Branch, with entrances into the Old and New Loco. Yards from the Up Branch line, to enable Loco. coal Trains and stores wagons to be shunted off and reach their destination without crossing into the passr. station. At present our passr. roads thro' the station are blocked daily for many hours with Trains of Loco. coal and Stores Wagons – this Box if fixed would prevent this state of things. *Since erected and evil remedied.*

A connection from Down Main to Down Branch is urgently required to enable vehicles to be transferred from Train to Train when standing at the platforms. At present the Down Main Line Trains must leave before we can commence to get the Boxes &c. in by the latter Trains – ready to attach to the Down Branch or Weymo. Trains. *This Connection has now been fixed.*

A Blow Pipe connection between the Booking Office at Swindon and the Tkt. Collectors stationed on the Up and Down platforms at the top of the Staircasees – particularly the Up side – is very much required to prevent passrs. being left behind after being booked.

The Town Goods shed is now urgently required to be removed from the vicinity of the passr. station and the whole of the Swindon Goods Staff should be brought together at the Transfer. The Highworth and also the Swindon, Marlboro' & Andover Cos. will shortly be opened to run into Swindon Station. We therefore require accommodation for short local Trains which at present does not exist. The short sidings east of the station must be cleared of Goods and arrangements for Bays to be made in which the local Trains can stand and start from. If the Goods shed is removed the Down Main Line platform and also the Down Branch platform should be extended 150 feet east of their present sites. The removal of the Goods would take up room now occupied by the thro' traffic. I would therefore suggest that the ground east of 'B' Box, lately occupied to hold marked-off broad gauge vehicles, now lying unoccupied, should be utilized for four narrow gauge Coal Trains of 40 wagons each. The Rails are on the ground (fixed broad gauge), all that is required would be the rails narrowed and ground levelled. *All the work since completed, for two roads.*

A panorama from the roof of the Down side station buildings, 1910, showing laden coal trucks outside the coal wharf, with the carpenters shop beyond. The junction of Sheppard Street and Gloucester Street is to the left, with the Mechanics' Institute and the water tower of the railway works just visible on the skyline

The renowned refreshment rooms at Swindon station, opened in 1842. Notorious for their high prices and inferior food, the lessees had the benefit of a compulsory 10-min stop by all trains at Swindon until 1895

GREAT WESTERN RAILWAY.

(2902 Amended).

Statement of PASSENGER, PARCELS and MISCELLANEOUS TRAFFIC at **Swindon June** Station.

Month **July** 1928

This Return must be sent to your Divisional Superintendent not later than the 8th of each Month, immediately after the Audit Office Accounts have been sent to Paddington.

MONTH	(1) Passengers Booked — By Rail — Ordinary Tickets First Class No.	Third Class No.	Cheaps and Excursion etc. No.	Total No.	By Road Motor Cars — Receipts £	Number	Receipts £	(2) Season Tickets Issued No.	£	(3) Excess Fares Collected No.	£	(4) Total Passenger Receipts £	(5) Various Receipts — Platform Tickets £	Registration of Seats £	Cab Rent £	Lavatories £	Other Receipts S. & Corn. £	(6) Total of Various Receipts £	(7) Total Passenger and Various Receipts £
This year's figures	204	7274	21594	29072	7663	–		29	103	–		7766	51		4	12·13·8	6·10·0	72	7838
Last year's figures	203	8991	22791	31985	8972	4333	128	26	94			9194	51	1	4	3·9·9	6·0·0	65	9259
Increase	1							3	9							9·3·11		7	
Decrease		1717	1197	2913	1309	4333	128					1428		1			2·10		1421

Brief explanation of Increase or Decrease in Passenger Receipts *Decrease in Works privilege tickets 1548 passenger 204. Road Motors now dealt with at Wantage Rd. Mechanics trip June 29th this year & July 1st last year: more booking included in June this year. August Bank Holiday Aug 1st last year & Aug 6 this year more holiday booking included in August a/c. this year*

MONTH	(8) Parcels Traffic — Forwarded Local and R.C.H. "Paid" and "To Pay" No.	Local Paid R.C.H. "Paid & To Pay" less Ons.	Received Local and R.C.H. "Paid" and "To Pay" No.	Local Paid R.C.H. "Paid & To Pay" less Ons.	(9) Horse, Carriage, Dog and Miscellaneous — Forwarded Local and R.C.H. "Paid" and "To Pay" No.	Local Paid R.C.H. "Paid & To Pay" less Ons.	Received Local and R.C.H. "Paid" and "To Pay" No.	Local "To Pay" R.C.H. "Paid & To Pay" less Ons.	(10) Total Parcels and Miscellaneous — Forwarded Local and R.C.H. "Paid" and "To Pay" No.	Local "Paid" R.C.H. "Paid & To Pay" less Ons.	Received Local and R.C.H. "Paid" and "To Pay" No.	Local "To Pay" R.C.H. "Paid & To Pay" less Ons.	(11) Total Coaching Receipts £	(12) Total Traffic Payroll Expenses £	(13) Milk Traffic Forwarded (included in Columns (9) and (10)) Cans No.	Receipts £
This year's figures	4835	427	11,557	484	1296	206	1554	172	6131	633	13,111	656	9127	3639	929	50
Last year's figures	4636	448	10,929	465	1062	305	1409	146	5701	753	12,338	611	10,623	3670	680	41
Increase	199		628	19	231		145	26	430		773	45			249	9
Decrease		21				99				120			1496	31		

Brief Explanation of Increase or Decrease in Parcels Receipts *(Forwarded) Less Bicycle, Pram etc (accompanied) traffic and less News traffic this year (Received) Increase Pigeon traffic*

Ditto Miscellaneous Receipts *(Forwarded) Less Horse traffic, less Motor Car traffic (Road Transport Dept), more milk this ye (Received) Increase in amount of extra cartage (Collection of Milk, Farm to Station*

Signature Station Master *R. Hooper* Date *Aug 13th* 1928

GREAT WESTERN RAILWAY

(2902 Amended).

Statement of PASSENGER, PARCELS and MISCELLANEOUS TRAFFIC at **Swindon Jn** Station.

Month **Septr** 1928

This Return must be sent to your Divisional Superintendent not later than the 8th each Month, immediately after the Audit Office Accounts have been sent to Paddington.

MONTH	(1) Passengers Booked — By Rail — Ordinary Tickets First Class No.	Third Class No.	Cheaps and Excursion etc. No.	Total No.	By Road Motor Cars — Receipts £	Number	Receipts £	(2) Season Tickets Issued No.	£	(3) Excess Fares Collected No.	£	(4) Total Passenger Receipts £	(5) Various Receipts — Platform Tickets £	Registration of Seats £	Cab Rent £	Lavatories £	Other Receipts S. & Corn. £	(6) Total of Various Receipts £	(7) Total Passenger and Various Receipts £
This year's figures	193	7467	22679	30339	6872	639	18	36	192			7082	61			15·9·2	2	78	7160
Last year's figures	191	8753	18572	27616	6696	5042	159	35	218			7073	56			13·9·11	2	71	7144
Increase	2		4107	1823	176			1				9	5					7	16
Decrease		1286				4403	141		26										

Brief explanation of Increase or Decrease in Passenger Receipts *Increase Works Priv tickets:- 879 Passeng £2. Increase in half Day & Day Excursion + Week End + Tourist tickets. Decrease in ordinary booking. Road Motors dealt with at Wantage Rd. Sep 24. Lambourn service off. North Wilts ...*

MONTH	(8) Parcels Traffic — Forwarded Local and R.C.H. "Paid" and "To Pay" No.	Local "Paid" R.C.H. "Paid & To Pay" less Ons.	Received Local and R.C.H. "Paid" and "To Pay" No.	Local "Paid" R.C.H. "Paid & To Pay" less Ons.	(9) Horse, Carriage, Dog and Miscellaneous — Forwarded Local and R.C.H. "Paid" and "To Pay" No.	Local "Paid" R.C.H. "Paid & To Pay" less Ons.	Received Local and R.C.H. "Paid" and "To Pay" No.	Local "To Pay" R.C.H. "Paid & To Pay" less Ons.	(10) Total Parcels and Miscellaneous — Forwarded Local and R.C.H. "Paid" and "To Pay" No.	Local "Paid" R.C.H. "Paid & To Pay" less Ons.	Received Local and R.C.H. "Paid" and "To Pay" No.	Local "To Pay" R.C.H. "Paid & To Pay" less Ons.	(11) Total Coaching Receipts £	(12) Total Traffic Payroll Expenses £	(13) Milk Traffic Forwarded (included in Columns (9) and (10)) Cans No.	Receipts £
This year's figures	3892	405	11683	480	1156	305	1351	199	5048	710	13034	679	8544	3663	859	48
Last year's figures	4246	452	12058	521	976	229	1563	168	5222	681	13621	689	8514	3687	664	38
Increase					180	76		31		29			35		195	10
Decrease	354	47	375	41			212		174		587	10		24		

Brief Explanation of Increase or Decrease in Parcels Receipts *Newspaper Labels down £10 + extra Sunday in month. Heavier Vels becoming Miscellaneous 2/c*

Ditto Miscellaneous Recpt *Horse Up heavier. Recd. Larger consignments + increase in cartage*

Signature Station Master *R. Hooper* Date *Oct 12th* 1928

GWR Statements of Passenger, Parcels and Miscellaneous Traffic at Swindon Junction, July and September 1928. These returns must have been the bane of station masters throughout the GWR as they struggled to find convincing reasons for sudden increases or decreases in traffic

Swindon station façade viewed
from Wellington Street (above)
and Station Road (right), 1960.
Structurally little had changed
since the 1910 photograph on
p. 115, and another thirteen
years were to elapse before the
demolition of this fine Georgian
building

The archetypal GWR signal
box: Swindon station west
box pictured from the end
of platform 4, 1960 (left)

The shabbiness of the station is highlighted in these two platform views from 1970. Platform 4 and all the Down side buildings were to be swept away within a few years as part of the station redevelopment, while on platform 3 only the ornate cast–iron veranda pillars have survived intact to this day

Swindon Shed

The original engine shed at Swindon was built in 1842 alongside the main London to Bristol line and at right angles to the adjoining repair shop. A new shed was built during the 1870s (above) on land between the Gloucester branch and the North Wilts Canal, at which time the former building was converted for locomotive repair purposes. The above view dates from the mixed gauge era, and is looking northwards, with the running sheds to the right and the stock sheds and gasworks to the left. The single-road broad gauge shed, used until the abolition of broad gauge in 1892, can be seen in the centre of the picture

Early 1930s view of the shed, with 'King' class engine No. 6000 *King George V* to the right

Panorama of coaling stage and shed approach roads, 1943. The Masons' Yard is in the foreground, with the silhouettes of the machine stores and St Augustine's Church discernible to the north-west

Swindon stock sheds and gasworks in decrepit condition, 1953. The engine is ex-M&SWJR No. 12 (built by Dübs in 1894) which was renumbered 1336 by the GWR and finally withdrawn in 1954. Swindon shed itself finally closed in 1964

Monitoring the performance of 'County' class No. 1009 *County of Carmarthen* during draughting experiments on the Locomotive Testing Plant in 'A' shop, 1950s. Note the distinctly un-Great Western flangeless chimney fitted to the engine

Unfortunately, the date and occasion of this superb portrait view are not known. Obviously some form of presentation had been made, while the men range from apprentices to retirees. The locomotive, 'Star' class No. 4036 *Queen Elizabeth* was built at Swindon in 1910 and withdrawn by British Railways in 1952

Enginemen and Firemen's Improvement Class, Swindon, 1907, posed in front of 'Saint' class No. 2903 *Lady of Lyons*. This and the photograph on the following page were both taken by the firm of A. Banbury, Faringdon Street, Swindon

Enginemen and Firemen's Improvement Class, Swindon, 1911, this time posed in front of two 'Saint' class locomotives adjacent to the running sheds. Behind the wooden valve-gear mock-up stands the young William Stanier, at that time Divisional Locomotive Superintendent and later to become Chief Mechanical Engineer of the LMS

Putting the finishing touches to 'Castle' class engine No. 4082 *Windsor Castle* at Swindon on 25 January 1936, prior to its hauling the funeral train of the late King George V from Paddington to Windsor three days later. The king 'drove' this engine during his visit to Swindon Works in 1924 (see p. 66)

'Castle' class No. 5055 *Lydford Castle*, newly-built, emerges on the traverser from the 'A' erecting shop, 1936, with accompanying fitters

A 'Castle' preserved: the handing-over ceremony of No. 4079 *Pendennis Castle* to the Great Western Society, April 1965. Those present include the former Chief Mechanical Engineer of the GWR, F.W. Hawksworth (centre), flanked by the Mayor of Swindon, Councillor Mervyn Webb, and the Chief Works Manager, J.S. Scott; also the Assistant Works Manager, A.A. Loveday (far left), Locomotive Works Manager, H.W. Mear (far right), and former Swindon railwaymen Reg Hanks (fourth from left) and John Dymond (third from right)

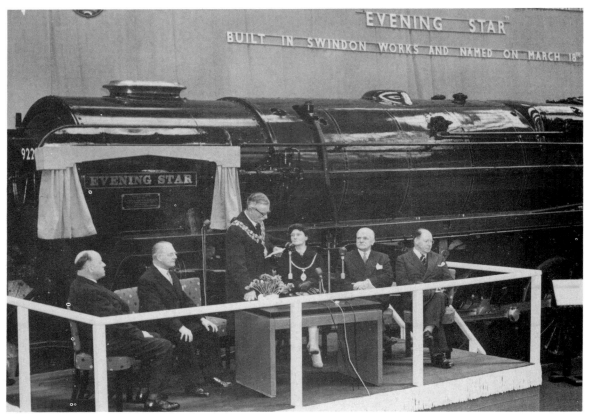

The naming ceremony of the last steam locomotive to be built by British Railways, No. 92220 *Evening Star*, in the 'A' Shop at Swindon, 18 March 1960. Above: the Mayor of Swindon, Councillor Frank Jefford, addresses the crowd; K.W.C. Grand, General Manager of British Railways (Western Region), who carried out the official unveiling of the *Evening Star* name-plate, and R.A. Smeddle, Chief Mechanical and Electrical Engineer, are seated to the far left and right respectively. Below: spectators at the ceremony, some utilizing the footplate and boiler of No. 6916 *Misterton Hall* to gain a better view

The 'Farewell to Steam' railtour at Swindon, November 1965: the Mayor, Councillor John Dymond, and the indefatigable Mr Hawksworth, then aged eighty-one, greet the driver of No. 7029 *Clun Castle* on platform 4

Acknowledgements

GWR Museum collection: pp. v, x, xii, 10, 11 lower, 18 lower left, 19, 20, 21, 23 upper left and upper right, 24, 25, 26 upper and lower, 27–41, 43, 44 upper left and upper right, 45, 46, 47 lower, 48 lower, 49, 50, 52 upper, 55, 56 upper left, 57, 58, 61, 62, 63, 66, 67, 68 upper, 69, 70, 71, 72, 73 upper, 82 top, 85 top and middle, 87, 88, 89, 90, 91, 92 upper, 93 lower, 94, 95 middle, 97 lower, 98, 99, 100, 103, 104 upper, 109 upper, 110 upper, 111, 112, 113, 114 upper, 117, 118 lower, 119, 123 upper, 124, 126, 127, 129 upper, 130. Swindon Reference Library collection: pp. 1–8, 12, 48 upper, 51, 54 upper, 75 upper, 76, 78, 79, 81 upper, 84 lower, 86, 93 upper, 95 top, 97 upper, 106 upper, 108, 122 upper, 128, 129 lower. Swindon Museum & Art Gallery collection: pp. 14 upper, 15, 16 upper left and lower, 18 upper, 22 lower, 44 lower, 64 middle, 65 upper. Wiltshire Newspapers: pp. 13, 52 lower, 56 upper right, 58 upper, 59, 60, 73 lower, 120, 121, 131. Geoff Parker collection: pp. 9 top and middle, 11 upper, 14 lower, 17, 22 upper, 23 lower, 54 lower, 65 lower, 101 upper, 102 lower, 105 lower, 106 lower, 107 upper left and upper right, 109 lower, 115 upper, 118 upper, 122 lower. Brian Hilton: pp. 83 lower, 84 upper, 85 bottom right, 92 lower, 95 bottom, 96, 123 lower. Richard Tomkins collection: pp. 75 lower, 77, 81 lower, 82 middle and bottom, 83 upper, 102 upper, 110 lower, 114 lower, 116. Fred Stevens collection: pp. 16 upper right, 64 top, 85 bottom left, 115 lower. N.E. Stead: p. 80. Mrs M. Underwood: p. 9 bottom. Mrs C. Tomkins: p. 74. Peter Sheldon: pp. 18 lower right, 42, 125. Richard Tomkins: pp. 47 upper, 53 lower, 56 lower left and lower right, 64 bottom. Denis Raven: pp. 53 upper, 104 lower, 105 upper right. Don Matthews: p. 68 lower. Original GWR and BR official photographs are reproduced by courtesy of the National Railway Museum and are Crown copyright. Broad gauge locomotive photographs on pp. 27–31 are reproduced by courtesy of Mr P.A. Nice. Material from the Swindon Museums collection is reproduced by courtesy of the Arts and Recreation Service of the Borough of Thamesdown.

For assistance in the preparation of this book, thanks are due to Tim Bryan (Keeper, Swindon Railway Museum), Robert Dickinson (Keeper, Swindon Museum & Art Gallery), John Woodward (Curator, Swindon Museums), Roger Trayhurn and the staff at Swindon Reference Library, Mrs Howell of Wiltshire Newspapers, Peter Clifford of Alan Sutton Publishing Limited, David Weston, and Tarmac Limited.

Bibliography

Gordon Coltas, *Names and Nameplates of the GWR*. (Heyday Publishing) 1985.
K.J. Cook, *Swindon Steam 1921–1951*. (Ian Allan) 1974.
Denis Griffiths, *Locomotive Engineers of the GWR*. (Patrick Stephens) 1987.
GWR Engines: Names, Numbers, Types and Classes. (David & Charles reprint) 1971.
E.T. MacDermot, *History of the Great Western Railway*. (GWR) 1927/1931.
Alan Peck, *The Great Western at Swindon Works*. (OPC) 1983.